Arthur's Garden

"I was simply entranced by this book; I could not put it down! What a delightful story of a man's love of his garden and how it penetrated the life of an ordinary family.

I am not given to tears, but I had more than a lump in my throat reading Arthur's Garden. It moved me very deeply and deserves a wide readership."

GEORGE CAREY, ARCHBISHOP OF CANTERBURY (1991–2002)

"What an enchanting book. Arthur's Garden is a charming, easy, and interesting read. It will bring back many different memories for many of us and perhaps enlighten younger readers of what times gone by were really like.

Sadly, I never had a delightful Great Uncle Arthur in my life, but I did have a dad who embarrassed us all by rushing out from our garden flat with a shovel to scoop up the horse droppings whenever the milk cart came by. How important our small London garden was to him; a life-long obsession and hobby. He and Arthur would have got along very well!"

VALERIE SINGLETON OBE, TELEVISION AND RADIO PRESENTER

"This is a heart-warming read, filled with delights. It is history told through the life of a small domestic garden and its owner, Arthur; a magical reflection on the part our gardens played through two major wars and during the aftermath. I found it a truly original idea, filled with nostalgic charm."

WENDY CRAIG, ACTOR, AUTHOR AND ENTERTAINER

"Pam brings to life Tom, Emily, and their nine children and, especially Arthur and his garden: the little patch of heaven that was all his own. It is here that he finds it easy to pray, echoing Dorothy Frances Gurney's words about being nearer to God's heart in a garden than anywhere else on earth.

Woven around their lives near Chatham Dockyard, we follow their ups and downs against a backdrop of major global events and delightful quotes ranging from Disraeli to Kipling, with the changing seasons of the garden always at its heart. A delightfully written book and beautifully illustrated. I loved it!"

REVD CINDY KENT MBE

Illustrations by SARA MULVANNY

PAM RHODES

Arthur's Garden

Up the Garden Path, Down Memory Lane

LION

Published by
Lion Hudson Limited
Wilkinson House, Jordan Hill Business Park
Banbury Road, Oxford OX2 8DR, England
www.lionhudson.com

Hardback ISBN 978 0 7459 8044 7

First edition 2019

Acknowledgments see p. 208

A catalogue record for this book is available from the British Library

Printed and bound in the UK, February 2019, LH55

I have so many wonderful memories of Uncle Arthur,
Uncle Wilf, Gran, Nan, Dad, and all those other unforgettable
characters from my down-to-earth, brave, funny, glorious family.
Gone now, but always remembered with love.

1906

I wonder if the Daffodil
Shrinks from the touch of frost,
And when her veins grow stiff and still
She dreams that life is lost?
Ah, if she does, how sweet a thing
Her resurrection day in spring!

Emma C. Dowd,
"Daffodil and Crocus"

THE DAFFODILS WERE out!

As Emily Freeman sat in the rocking chair on that early April morning, she smiled to see the trumpet flowers turning their golden faces towards the early morning sun. With the frost still on their handkerchief-sized lawn, and a cold wind whipping down the row of terraced houses, those daffodils seemed so courageous and bright. Her husband Tom knew they'd always been her favourite flowers, and added a few more bulbs every year just for her.

A snuffling noise and slight movement from the baby in her arms caught her attention, and she looked down at the crumpled, frowning face peering out from the crocheted shawl in which she'd nursed six babies before this one. She didn't include in that number her firstborn son Thomas, who'd only managed a few hours of life before he simply stopped breathing – nor Alice, the tiny twin who'd been stillborn four years later, the painfully thin little girl who seemed to have given all her strength to her much more robust sister, Ada. Now a strapping six-year-old, Ada would love this new addition to the family. Like her big sister Lily, the oldest of their children at the age of nine, Ada loved playing "mum" to each new baby as it came along. And now there was Arthur – a nice traditional name. Emily liked that.

Mind you, space was going to be tight. She and Tom now had to squeeze six children into the three-bedroomed terraced house that Tom had managed to find for them when they'd married just over a decade earlier. Queen Victoria had been on the throne then. Five years after her death, how different things felt now – a change of century to welcome in an exciting new era as her son Edward took the throne.

Of course, King Edward would have plenty of room for his growing family at Buckingham Palace! Tom and Emily's home, typical of so many rows of terraced houses up and down the country, was packed to the rafters. As soon as he was old enough, Arthur would be joining the boys in the front bedroom – Ernest aged eight, Dick, four, and little John who was coming up to two years old – while next door in the box room, the girls, Lily and Ada, topped and tailed in a single bed.

A smile crept across Emily's face. Tightly packed they may be in a home that was filled with a muddle of children – with all their chatter, wailing, giggles and tussles – but somehow they managed to scrape along, making Tom's meagre pay packet from his job in Chatham Dockyard stretch to keep food on the table and clothes on their backs. The daily grind of constant work and the sharp edges of family life were smoothed and buffered by the loving bond between them all.

Love? Emily chuckled to herself at the very thought. Tom and she never spoke of love. They didn't need to. They weren't sentimental like that. For heaven's sake, even after all these children Tom had never seen her with her clothes off and the lights on! That wouldn't do at all.

But as little Arthur snuggled back to sleep in her arms, Emily's heart lurched with fondness when she glanced out of the window to see Tom pushing his battered old wheelbarrow down the garden path as he headed for the vegetable patch. Those vegetables were a family necessity all year round, but Emily suspected it wasn't Tom's green fingers that kept him out in the garden. With a house full of youngsters, that was the quietest place to be: a little patch of heaven that was all his own.

The year's at the spring,
And day's at the morn;
Morning's at seven;
The hill-side's dew-pearl'd;
The lark's on the wing;
The snail's on the thorn;
God's in His Heaven –
All's right with the world!

Robert Browning,
from **Pippa Passes**

Tom held his face up to the wind and wondered whether he should
be planting seeds today. He knew what his old grandad would have
said: "Take off your trousers and sit on the ground. You'll soon
know if the soil's warm enough."

Tom chuckled to himself. That would give Mrs Edwards two
doors up something to complain about. Not that she needed much
help to do that. But then, Mrs Edwards was definitely an "old wife"
and surely the idea of gardeners testing cold soil with their bare
bottoms was a tale "old wives" loved to tell!

And his grandad certainly wasn't an "old wife", yet he'd often
told Tom when he was a boy that there was truth in the rumour

that the very best of Queen Victoria's under-gardeners could be found in early spring squatting bare-bottomed in the palace kitchen garden, their faces a picture of deep concentration. After all, their jobs relied on the success of the harvest, and it was a known fact that if seeds were sown before the cold, wet spring weather was over, the ground might not have had chance to warm up, and the crops could fail.

Oh, Grandad loved telling tales like that. Tom smiled to himself as he recalled how the old man, right up to his dying day, always had a line of ancient wisdom at the ready to pass on to his grandson – especially if it involved anything that grew in, flew over or nibbled at his garden. The trouble was that his hand-me-down lines of advice often seemed to Tom to be at odds with each other.

"Remember, son," he'd say, his rheumy eyes narrowing dramatically as he looked out over his vegetable patch, "the rule in gardening, never forget, is to sow dry and set wet!"

Then, as Tom dutifully waited for the spring sunshine to warm up the ground a little so that he could "sow dry", his grandad would suddenly appear at his elbow, shielding his eyes as he peered up towards the sky. Eventually he would shake his head gravely, turning to Tom to make the pronouncement: "Never sow seeds when the moon is waning."

It was all very confusing for young Tom, but those years spent pottering around the garden with Grandad had stood him in good stead for the man he'd become. Take planting seeds, for example. Tom could still hear the voice of his grandfather saying:

Sow seeds a-plenty all in a row,
One for the rook, one for the crow,
One to rot and one to grow.

So, thanks to Grandad, Tom always had a plentiful supply of seeds at the ready, kept and dried from the year before. Each autumn, he'd wait until their pods began to dry out and crack open, then he'd lay the seed heads on blotting paper and cover them with an old muslin cloth to stop them blowing away. They'd be left for a month or more before he checked to see if they were dry enough by putting them in an airtight glass jar, which he placed in a nice warm spot. If he saw any condensation inside the jar, he'd take the seeds out to let them dry for a week or so longer. When he was sure they were ready, he would pop different varieties into small brown envelopes, each carefully labelled, ready for planting out the following spring. Most of the seeds Tom grew every year were descended from the plants Grandad had grown, like his father before him. *After all, thought Tom, why bother to change when you've already found the best?*

> *Whether the weather be cold*
> *Or whether the weather be hot,*
> *Whatever the weather,*
> *We'll weather the weather,*
> *Whether we like it or not!*

Tom looked back towards the house to catch sight of his wife sitting at the back bedroom window in the rocking chair, probably nursing Arthur. He gave her a cheery wave before picking up his snippers from the wheelbarrow, and heading towards the back fence. The ivy there was out of control after the long winter months, and needed a good prune before the summer arrived.

As he snipped, he found himself humming the melody from a song he and Emily had heard at the music hall on their anniversary outing three years earlier. In the story of the song, these words were said by a young girl to her grandfather, but whenever Tom heard the chorus, it made him think of his own wife. He and Emily were the practical kind, sleeves rolled up as they worked their way through all the jobs that had to be done each day. They'd always been easy company for each other – and yet, was that enough? If it was romance she wanted, he wouldn't know where to begin. All he knew was that he couldn't imagine life without her. Just like that ivy, their lives were comfortably entwined together, deep rooted and strong.

Granddad sat at evenfall
'Neath the dear old garden wall
Where the ivy was clinging all around
And a maiden young and fair
With blue eyes and golden hair
Was nestling there beside him on the ground.
"Some day you'll be leaving me
For a sweetheart," the old man sighed.
"Some day be forgetting me."
But with a smile the maid replied

"Just watch the ivy on that old garden wall
Clinging so tightly, what e'er may befall.
As you grow older I'll be constant and true
And just like the ivy, I'll cling to you."

"When the ivy, years ago,"
Said the maiden, "Began to grow,
Then that wall supported it with pride.
Now the old wall's in decay
And is crumbling fast away
The ivy clings more tightly to its side.
Loving, you have ever been,
You have cared for me day by day.
Loving, I shall ever be,
And always by your side I'll stay."

**Arthur J. Mills and Harry Castling,
"Just Like the Ivy"**

1911

Show me your garden and I shall tell you what you are.

Alfred Austin

In 1911, the day Arthur turned five merited a celebration that was so much more than just a birthday. That was the day he was breeched, a rite of passage that made him feel proud beyond words. He was a big boy at last, no longer wearing the traditional smock that all little boys wore until they reached the grand old age of five, when they were declared grown up enough to wear proper breeches. There was old-fashioned common sense behind this custom for most families in their corner of Kent. After all, a smock allowed for sudden spurts of growth. It could be handed down from big brother to new baby – and, most important of all, it allowed easy access. Every mother was grateful for the smock during those long months, sometimes years, during which their toddler had not quite got the hang of potty training!

A new little sister had been added to the family since Arthur was born. Now just over two years old, Elsie had bright blue eyes and a mass of pale golden curls that tumbled over her shoulders. She adored Arthur and followed him everywhere. Not today though, he thought, turning to tell Elsie sternly that Mother wanted her back in the house. Today Arthur would be playing with the big boys. Today he was wearing trousers!

Arthur grinned as he saw his very best friend clambering over their side fence to join him. Wilf was the boy next door, six months younger and already two inches taller than Arthur, with a crop of dark red hair and a face full of freckles. On most days, Wilf and Arthur would hang about together in one of their gardens – usually Wilf's because there was less danger of doing damage to flowers and vegetables there than in Arthur's family garden. Wilf's dad had a happily relaxed attitude to life. He laughed a lot, probably because he liked beer a lot too, and he didn't think much about practicalities like paying bills, keeping house or digging gardens. It drove Wilf's mum to distraction, but all the nagging in the world wouldn't change him. Arthur once heard his own dad, Tom, muttering under his breath about his irresponsible neighbour:

As is the garden, such is the gardener. A man's nature runs either to herbs or weeds.

Francis Bacon, "Of Nature in Men"

When it came to growing weeds, Wilf's dad was an expert.

For Arthur and Wilf, though, a garden wasn't meant to be useful. It was there for fun. The two boys spent long afternoons wading through Wilf's garden, knee-high in grass, or hanging over the fence which, like all the gardens at the back of their row of terraced houses, looked out across a dusty pathway on to the coal depot below. There was always something to watch there: lorries arriving to be met by a small army of men carrying huge black sacks of coal on their shoulders, ready to line them up on each truck so that it could be on its way again.

But on Arthur's birthday, Wilf had been invited to join the family for a special birthday tea. The two boys made their way back into the house just as the family were taking their seats around the table set with mouth-watering favourites: thick-cut sandwiches filled with bloater paste or Mother's own strawberry jam; red jelly with a big bowl of pink blancmange which had been set in one of his mum's largest pudding bowls; and a sugary jam sponge lovingly made by his big sister Lily, with five candles on top that Arthur managed to blow out with just one puff.

There was salad too, proudly brought into the kitchen by Arthur's dad who, for weeks, had kept a paraffin heater going in the glass "lean-to" that was his home-made version of a proper greenhouse. Because of it, for most of the year, he was able to provide a few lettuces, spring onions and radishes for special occasions like this. Emily had arranged a big round plate in circles of colour made from lettuce and tomato, alongside dishes of home-made pickled onions and green apple chutney. There were hard-boiled eggs too, a donation from Fred up the road who kept chickens. Each day, his cockerel woke the whole street up at five in the morning, and many an old boot had been thrown in its direction from a nearby bedroom window by a disgruntled mother who'd just got her baby off to sleep. All that was forgotten, though, as everyone tucked into the feast before singing "Happy Birthday" to a big boy who was five!

> *Yes! in the poor man's garden grow*
> *Far more than herbs and flowers –*
> *Kind thoughts, contentment, peace of mind,*
> *And joy for weary hours.*

Mary Howitt, "The Poor Man's Garden"

1914

*... there are for many of us three gardens: the garden
outdoors, the garden of pots and bowls in the house, and
the garden of the mind's eye.*

Katharine S. White, "Onward and Upward in the Garden"

The diamond shapes in the heavy cut-glass vase caught the sunlight
as Emily carefully arranged the stems of purple lilac blossoms into
this treasured family heirloom, a gift to her own mother and father
on the day they were married. Throughout the whole year, Mother
had always kept the vase filled with a colourful display that sat in
pride of place on a lace doily in the middle of the sideboard in the
front parlour, a room kept for "best" so that, unless visitors came, it
was rarely used. Daffodils and tulips would be followed by peonies
and roses as the summer flowers began to fill the garden, then
asters and dahlias, with chrysanths and autumn berries next, until
in December the elegant vase graced the middle of their Christmas
table draped with shining holly leaves
and wisps of trailing ivy.

There is no season such delight can bring
As summer, autumn, winter and the spring!

William Browne, from Britannia's Pastorals: Book II

The round-the-year pleasure of bringing the garden into their home was a custom Emily loved to follow, and as usual, once she'd chosen the flowers, she stood in the yard so that she could arrange them on the old kitchen table that stood just opposite the coal house door. The simple act of filling the vase always brought back memories of Mother doing exactly the same thing. Her father had been a typical Victorian husband, aloof and disappointingly distant towards his children. Emily smiled as she remembered how her mother was the complete opposite. Although she did her best to play the part of the stern Victorian mama, her naturally sunny nature and her inclination to giggle with delight at the sheer joy of her children, made her the most warm and loving of parents. Sadly, the consumption which claimed her life before she was even forty meant that although Mother saw Emily married, she didn't live long enough to meet any of her growing family of grandchildren.

Emily sighed. She still missed her mum and thought of her every day. Still, time was a healer. It was now 1914, and apart from Tom and herself, there were nine children living in the house – every one of them in the garden in front of her at that moment.

Baby Bo was six months old. When he'd been born at the end of October the previous year, two-year-old Harry had been unable to pronounce the baby's real name, Robert. At the time, Harry's favourite game was "peek-a-boo", so he just called his newborn brother Bo – and the name had stuck.

Elsie, the next eldest at five years old, was a bossy little madam who no longer took any interest in babies because she preferred playing chase with the boys, even though they kept trying to lose her. Whenever she went to hide, they'd make a point of not looking for her – until she reappeared to kick in the shin whichever brother she caught, shouting at him that she was going to play anyway, so there!

Arthur, now a solid, gentle eight-year-old who was the spitting image of his father, didn't mind Elsie tagging along with him. Mind you, she quickly got bored when all Arthur wanted to do was get out the hoe to do a bit of weeding. He'd always been a boy who enjoyed being outdoors getting his hands dirty, although Emily suspected that what he loved most of all was the chance to follow his dad around the garden being given instructions on the jobs of the day – like picking the caterpillars off the cabbages, collecting the ash from the fireplace to put around the roses, and spreading the leaves from the big brown teapot in the kitchen as mulch for the camellias. And every Friday night, Arthur stood alongside the tin bathtub as his father took first turn in the hot water. As soon as Dad had clipped his toenails, it was Arthur's job to collect up the nail clippings and take them out to the garden.

"Put them near the roots of the ceanothus," his dad would call after him. "They thrive on hoof and horn!"

Arthur is a good boy, thought Emily fondly, as she watched her children in the garden that afternoon.

"Look, Harry!" whispered Arthur, crouching down to pull the toddler onto his knee. Elsie, who hated the thought of missing out on anything, immediately came across to find out what they were looking at.

"There's that robin again! See, just there on the fence?"

"There, silly!" Elsie jabbed her finger in the direction of the tall fence running alongside where her mother was working.

Harry's face lit up. "Wobin!"

"Not Wobin," corrected Elsie with exaggerated patience. "Robin! It starts with an 'r'. Can you do that, Harry? Can you say 'robin'?"

"Wobin!" beamed Harry triumphantly. "Wobin!"

"Wobin it is then," grinned Arthur, as Elsie stomped off in a huff.

Ada, a rather shy fourteen-year-old, was sitting on the wall that was supposed to stop children tripping into their little pond, talking to their eldest girl, Lily. At seventeen, Lily was just becoming aware of how pretty she was with her dark blonde hair and blue eyes. Under her parents' watchful eye, she had started walking out with Laurie, a young man who had recently begun working with her father in the dockyard. *How young she looks*, thought Emily. *She's little more than a child.* Had her own mother thought the same about her when she'd walked down the aisle with Tom three months after her seventeenth birthday?

The older boys – John who was ten, Dick twelve, and Ernest who, now he was sixteen, was trying rather unsuccessfully to grow a moustache that apparently was the height of fashion for stylish young men – were all leaning over the fence at the bottom of the garden, looking out across the path towards the coal depot below. It was Sunday, so the depot was thankfully quiet, and Emily could hear the different tones of her sons' voices as they drifted back to her down the length of the garden. John still sounded high pitched, like the young boy he was. Dick's voice was on the point of breaking, squeaking one moment and growling the next. Ernest, though, had inherited his clear tenor voice from Tom. Often, as the family gathered round the piano to pick favourites from the Ira Sankey hymn book, or popular songs they all knew, father and son would choose to sing a duet together. Their particular favourite was that beautiful old ballad "The Last Rose of Summer". Their rendition was so heartfelt that it never failed to bring tears to Emily's eyes.

She shivered. Were her family also coming to the end of a kind of summer, with its peaceful days they'd always taken for granted? The papers were full of the tension building up between Britain, along with its allies France and Russia, and the German Empire, with Austria-Hungary and Italy. Who knew where that could lead?

She looked across to Ernest, her strong, handsome, sensitive son, and shuddered.

How many million Aprils came
Before I ever knew
How white a cherry bough could be,
A bed of squills, how blue.

And many a dancing April
When life is done with me,
Will lift the blue flame of the flower
And the white flame of the tree.

Oh, burn me with your beauty, then,
Oh, hurt me, tree and flower,
Lest in the end death try to take
Even this glistening hour...

Sara Teasdale, "Blue Squills"

1916

Come, my love, and do not spurn
From a little flower to learn:
See the lily on the bed
Hanging down its modest head;
While it scarcely can be seen,
Folded in its leaf of green.

Yet we love the lily well,
For its sweet and pleasant smell,
And would rather call it ours
Than many other gayer flowers;
Pretty lilies seem to be
Emblems of humility.

'Tis not beauty that we prize,
Like a summer flower it dies.
But humility will last,
Fair and sweet, when beauty's past;
And the Saviour, from above,
Views a humble child with love.

Come, my love, and do not spurn
From a little flower to learn:
Let your temper be as sweet
As the lily at your feet;
Be as gentle, be as mild:
Be a modest, simple child.

Author unknown,
"The Lily of the Valley"

"ID HE GO DOWN on one knee?" Elsie demanded to know as she and Lily hung over the back fence. "If he wasn't down on his knees, the proposal doesn't count!"

"He certainly did," answered Lily dreamily. "It was all so romantic. Laurie had gone to so much trouble to make it a special evening for me. I mean, getting tickets for *The Tramp*. They're like gold dust!"

"I want to see that film," said Ada. "I've heard Charlie Chaplin is really good."

"Well, he doesn't say a word, but I still nearly split my sides laughing all the same," agreed Lily. "But he's a Londoner, isn't he – grew up there. He'd *have* to have a sense of humour!"

"Forget about the film!" interrupted Elsie. "How did Laurie propose? What did he say?"

Lily smiled at the memory. "Well, it could all have gone wrong really. I mean, it's February, freezing cold, and when we came out of that nice warm cinema, Laurie wanted us to walk up to the bridge – you know, the one over the river where the wind always catches your skirt if you're not careful."

"So what did you say to that?" asked Ada.

"I told him in no uncertain terms that I intended to get the half past nine bus and be home in front of the fire before my toes got frostbite."

"But he persuaded you?"

"Well, he always was good at cuddles," giggled Lily. "He wrapped me inside his coat, put his arm around my shoulders, and marched me up to the bridge anyway. Said I needed the exercise after sitting down all evening. The cheek of the man! But then, when we got to the middle of the bridge, he suddenly pulled away from me, fumbled for something in his pocket, dropped down on his knee, held out the box with the ring in it and asked me to do him the honour of becoming his wife!"

"And what did you say?" demanded Elsie.

"Yes, of course! I said yes, yes, yes – and that was that. We're engaged!"

Emily and Tom, who were sitting on the old bench by the shed while Tom filled his pipe, couldn't help but overhear the girls' conversation.

"Did you know this was coming?" asked Emily before taking a sip from her mug of tea.

He grinned. "Laurie came and asked me for permission to wed Lily about a week ago, but wanted me to keep it to myself. He's a good lad. After all, he's been my apprentice at the dockyard for more than two years now. I know he'll provide well for her."

"Can I be a bridesmaid?" demanded Elsie, throwing her arms around Lily's waist.

"Of course you can."

"When?"

"I'm not sure," Lily replied as the girls walked back up the garden towards where their parents were sitting. "Laurie's got quite a bit put by, but we'll still need to save up. Weddings aren't cheap."

"Where will you live?" asked Tom.

"We'd like our own house, of course, but I can't see how we'll manage that. Laurie says we can live with his mother when we first get wed."

"But she's old!" Elsie frowned with distaste.

"Laurie's mum is only a few years older than me, I'll have you know," said Emily firmly, "and that's a very kind offer she's made. Now she's on her own in that house, she'd probably like a bit of company."

Lily didn't reply.

"Well, this calls for a celebration!" announced Tom, knocking the ash from his pipe into the flowerbed as he abruptly got to his feet. He walked through the kitchen to the back room where the boys were playing cards, and called out, "Come and give me a hand, Dick. I'm sure we've got a bottle or two down in the cellar of that elderflower champagne Mother brewed up last year. John, you get the glasses – and Arthur, can you organize everyone to move into the parlour?"

It had to be the parlour, because that was the only room suitable for such a special occasion – to toast the happiness of bride and groom.

"To Lily and Laurie!" announced Tom, holding his glass high. "After two years of misery when the only news anyone talks about is this awful war, the thought of a wedding – the first in our family – brings us all great hope and joy. May God bless them with much happiness and a bright future together. May they live long and well!"

"Cheers!" shouted everyone. "Hip hip hurray!"

"You'll be next!" said Ada, who often seemed much older and wiser than her sixteen years. Ernest turned towards her with a grin.

"What makes you think that?"

"Oh, you're lovelorn over Millie. We can all see that."

He shook his head in agreement. "That obvious, eh?"

"So? What are you going to do about it?"

Ernest lowered his voice so that only Ada could hear. "I am going to ask her – of course I am. I've told her so too. I thought I'd do it on my eighteenth birthday at the end of March. That will give me a bit more time to get the money together for the ring."

Ada smiled with delight. "That's wonderful, Although Millie's far too good for you – you know that!"

"She doesn't think so, I'm glad to say," replied Ernest, his expression suddenly serious. "I don't know what she sees in me, but she seems to love me. I'm a lucky man."

Ada gave her big brother a hug. "She's the lucky one, to be spending her life with you!"

Just a few weeks later, the papers were full of the news that the Military Service Act 1916 had been passed. All single men between the ages of eighteen and forty-one were to be conscripted into the army with immediate effect. The war in France couldn't be won without them.

The day after his eighteenth birthday, Ernest signed up.

After that news about Ernest, none of the family felt much like celebrating Arthur's tenth birthday, which was just a week later. So, on his birthday, instead of walking straight home after school, Arthur made his way down to the bank of the River Medway. There, after several minutes, he spied what he was looking for. The flat circle of stone sat neatly in the palm of his hand – just the right size.

Once home, he took himself down to the bottom of the garden and sat on the bench in the small clearing beside the shed. Over the days that followed, he spent many hours there cleaning, polishing, buffing and engraving, until finally the little stone looked as he hoped it would.

He glanced up to see Wobin (or son of son of son of "Wobin" named by Bo all those years ago) on the fence beside him, his head cocked quizzically to one side. Arthur held out his hand to show the bird what he'd made.

"It's for Ernest, Wobin. It says 'Come Home'. I've poured my prayers into it. This stone will bring him back to us."

These dear little blossoms of dainty blue
Say please take care as I'm thinking of you,
Remember I love you, I'm faithful and true,
From one who, though distant, will not forget you.

Millie had never been a girl for needlework, but this verse embroidered in the middle of one of her soft linen handkerchiefs was a task she undertook with a mixture of love and fear. For two years, they'd already seen so many fine young men, including her own brother, march off to this "war to end all wars" – except there was no end in sight. It was getting worse. And now her beloved Ernest was going too. So she worked long into the night until her eyes and fingers ached, embroidering in bright blue, green and yellow cottons a ring of tiny forget-me-nots encircling the lines of poetry that had formed in her heart.

And that morning, with the feel of his uniform rough against her wet cheek, she clung to him, desperate with dread and fear, determined not to show it. Ernest needed to be strong. So did she.

At last, she stood at the gate with his family around her, his mother's arm linked through hers as they watched him walk away.

Ernest didn't look back. He couldn't. In his pocket, his fingers brushed against Arthur's carved stone as they closed around the precious handkerchief. Then, with his head erect and his eyes almost blinded by tears, he marched to the top of the road and out of sight.

Five months later in Flanders, for the very first time the British introduced tanks to the battlefield. For seven days at Flers-Courcelette on the Somme, the Allies fought for their lives against the Germans – until finally, on the 22nd September 1916, the British were declared victorious.

Ernest didn't know that. Twenty-four hours earlier, in one of the final rallies of that battle, he had fallen in No-Man's Land. He never came home again.

In Flanders fields the poppies blow
Between the crosses, row on row,
That mark our place; and in the sky
The larks, still bravely singing, fly
Scarce heard amid the guns below.

We are the Dead. Short days ago
We lived, felt dawn, saw sunset glow,
Loved and were loved, and now we lie
In Flanders fields.

Take up our quarrel with the foe:
To you from failing hands we throw
The torch; be yours to hold it high.
If ye break faith with us who die
We shall not sleep, though poppies grow
In Flanders fields.

John McCrae, "In Flanders Fields"

This is an odd sort of funeral, thought Emily, *with no coffin and no body to bury.* Her Ernest, her firstborn, her most loved and cherished son – his body lay broken and left in the land where he fell. There had been no prayers said for him there. How could there be? Who would care enough to pray over one young soldier dead on foreign soil when there were so many thousands of others? So those prayers had to be said here and now, in the church where he'd been baptized; where she and his father had married; where Ernest had planned to make Millie his wife.

With all her children around her, Emily managed to hold on to her dignity right up until the moment when Tom stepped up to the front and started to sing. How many times had she heard Ernest's fine tenor voice joining his father's to sing the old ballad they'd always loved?

'Tis the last rose of summer
Left blooming alone;
All her lovely companions
Are faded and gone;
No flower of her kindred,
No rosebud is nigh,
To reflect back her blushes,
To give sigh for sigh.

I'll not leave thee, thou lone one!
To pine on the stem;
Since the lovely are sleeping,
Go, sleep thou with them.
Thus kindly I scatter
Thy leaves o'er the bed,
Where thy mates of the garden
Lie scentless and dead.

So soon may I follow,
When friendships decay,
And from Love's shining circle
The gems drop away.
When true hearts lie withered

And fond ones are flown,
Oh! Who would inhabit
This bleak world alone?

Thomas Moore, "The Last Rose of Summer"

From his seat behind her, Arthur watched as his mother's shoulders heaved with sobs. *I poured my prayers into that stone*, he thought. *I asked God to save him. If God couldn't answer a prayer as important as that, what's the point of praying? He never listens.*

Later that week, Arthur helped Tom dig a hole beside their garden fence into which his father placed a very special rose. Mother stood flanked by Dick who, at fourteen, was now her eldest son, alongside John who was two years younger, while the smaller children, Elsie, Harry and Bo, were cared for by older sisters Lily and Ada.

"This is for Ernest," said Tom. "Every year when this rose blooms, we will remember him as we knew him, glorious and strong."

By July the following year, 1917, that bush had climbed enough to cover much of the fence with fragrant white roses.

Those roses were at the heart of the bouquet Lily carried down the aisle when she married Laurie. As more and more men were called to the Front, it seemed to the young couple that time was too precious to waste. She constantly gave thanks for the day Laurie had decided to follow the local tradition and get a job in Chatham Dockyard, because the ship building and maintenance work that went on there was so vital to the war effort that highly skilled men like her new husband were giving great service to their country.

The newly-marrieds moved in around the corner, to Laurie's family home where his widowed mother still lived thirty years after arriving there as a bride herself. And as the guns fell silent on the 11th November 1918 at the end of the First World War, Tom and Emily's first grandchild was born. He was named Ronald, after Laurie's father, and Ernest, after the big brother Lily would always love and remember with pride.

1922

Summer makes me drowsy. Autumn makes me sing.
Winter's pretty lousy, but I hate Spring.

Dorothy Parker, "Ethereal Mildness"

One late spring morning four years later in 1922, Wilf was stretched out on the small bench alongside the shed in Arthur's garden.

"I don't get it," he mused. "I know Dick's moved up to London for work now, and John's got that job at the gasworks, but Harry and Bo could help a lot more in the garden. After all, Harry is a big strapping lad for an eleven-year-old! Why doesn't your dad ask *them* to help out in the garden instead of you all the time?"

"He doesn't ask. I offer," replied Arthur, keeping up a steady rhythm as he hoed around the cabbage plants. "I like pottering about here and watching everything grow."

Wilf snorted with disbelief. "But you're sixteen. You're working as a chippy in the dockyard from seven o'clock every morning. You give just about all your wages to your mother. You only have the weekends to unwind a bit, and you spend most of that time digging around in your own back yard!"

"Well, Dad's not so well since he had that fall. He can't manage the heavy digging any more, and I really don't mind giving a hand."

"Come and have a drink with the boys tonight!"

"I've got work in the morning."

"So have I."

Arthur grinned. "Two hours sweeping up after the market's closed is hardly work! When are you going to get a proper job?"

"When my mum's better. She needs me to help her at home now that Dad's gone."

"Couldn't Beattie do that? Surely your mum would prefer to be looked after by her daughter rather than her son? After all, you're hardly house-trained, are you!"

"I don't think Beattie's husband would like that. Alf likes the tin bath filled and his tea on the table the moment he gets back from work. He'd not take kindly to Beattie's attention being taken elsewhere, even for our mum."

"That works well for you then!" chuckled Arthur as he rested the hoe against the fence and opened the shed door.

"Is bath night still Friday at your house?" Wilf asked after a while.

"That's right. As soon as we've filled the tub, Dad's in first, then Dick and Harry if they're home. Ada's next, then me – and after Harry and Bo are ready for bed, if there's any hot water left, Mum will go in."

"And does your mum still insist on you all lining up for a spoonful of castor oil?"

"Friday night every week! She says it keeps us regular…"

Wilf spluttered with laughter. "No wonder there's always a long queue for the privy in your back yard on Saturday mornings then!"

Suddenly his expression turned to one of horror. "Hey! What are you doing?"

Arthur looked back at his friend with surprise. "Giving the cabbages a drink."

"But that's beer you're pouring on them!"

"It's just the dregs from Dad's home-made brew. Cabbages love beer. It makes them grow."

"Well, I'm a growing chap," moaned Wilf. "Don't waste that beer on cabbages!"

Arthur grinned as he wiped his hands on his trousers. "I'm done here now," he said. "Want to walk up to the stable with me?"

"Whatever for?"

"I need some manure for the strawberries."

Wilf's face puckered up with disgust. "Euck! We'd rather have tinned cream on ours…"

1925

"Look, on the fence – there's Wobin!"

As he spoke, Bo grinned over towards Elsie, knowing how, even after all these years, it still irritated her when he pronounced the name incorrectly – as the whole family did!

The weather was surprisingly warm for just after Easter, but in that year of 1925, Easter had been late, well into April, so the garden was ablaze with the colours and scents of spring flowers and early blossom.

Bo, who was still thought of as the baby of the family even though he would be twelve in October that year, looked more like his big brother Arthur than any of his other siblings. Like Arthur, he enjoyed being outside, sometimes helping in the garden – although perhaps not today! It was Monday, washing day, and Mother had lit the geyser in the scullery well before breakfast. Six or more buckets of hot water were needed to get the wash going – and by mid-morning half the clothes line was filled with flapping pinafore dresses, camisoles and bloomers, trousers and shirts. Meanwhile, Mother soldiered on feeding sheets and pillow cases through the mangle to make them as dry as possible before taking them into the house to air in front of the fire.

Elsie, who considered herself a woman of the world now she was sixteen, shot Bo a look of irritation as he watched her struggling to hang one of the heavy sheets up on the swaying line.

"If you're not going to be useful, Bo, then clear out of my way! Better still, go and give Mother a hand with the mangle. She looks worn out."

"I wish I could help more," sighed their father, Tom, who was watching them from a wicker chair just outside the kitchen door.

"You have an excuse for not pulling your weight," pronounced

Elsie haughtily. "That back of yours can't take any strain at all since that fall you had. But Bo is just lazy!"

"Everyone knows washing is a woman's work!" announced Bo, immediately ducking down to avoid the wet flannel he thought Elsie might throw at him.

"I'll have you know that a woman is worth two of any man!" she snapped. "Women did all the men's jobs during the war and still managed to bring up their families single-handed. Can you think of even one man you know who could do that? And the men just waltzed back home expecting to push women aside to take those jobs again – in 1918, the same year women got the vote! That's seven years ago, so it's about time dinosaurs like you kept your antiquated, chauvinistic opinions to yourself!"

"What does chauvinistic mean?" asked Bo, his face a picture of innocence.

"It means you're taking on a full-blown argument you won't win," laughed Arthur, stepping out of the kitchen with a tin mug of tea for his father. "Not when Elsie's on her high horse about women's rights."

"Don't you start!" snapped Elsie.

"Whoa! I happen to agree with you. I mean, look at you, a typist in a solicitor's office."

"And that's all I'll ever be, if you men have your way. All those snide remarks about women taking up ex-servicemen's jobs, and how we're only good for domestic service!"

"Well, I could never do a job like yours," soothed Arthur who, with so many women in the house, had learned very early on how to smooth ruffled feathers.

"You'd just like to be a full-time gardener with someone else paying your wages to do what you love," retorted Elsie.

"That would be nice," agreed Arthur, "but I'd never get anywhere near as much as I do as a carpenter in the dockyard – and since Dad's accident, we certainly need every penny, especially as so many men are being laid off now there are no warships to build. No, gardening's just a hobby for me."

"Well, I envy you," said Tom, sipping his tea. "I feel like an old crock now with this gammy back, but inside me there'll always be a young gardener who's just itching to get my boots on and those weeds out."

"How can you tell which are weeds and which are flowers?" asked Bo.

"Try pulling one out," replied Tom. "If they come away easily, they're plants. Weeds will fight you every inch of the way."

"Anyway, Arthur," said Elsie as casually as she could, "you'll be nineteen soon. At your age, shouldn't you be sowing wild oats rather than planting cabbage seeds? I know Mary at the corner shop has her eye on you. Are you just playing hard to get?"

Arthur flushed with embarrassment. "I haven't got time for girls," he mumbled.

"Is it because you can't dance, Arthur?" asked Elsie. "I can do a ripping Charleston, you know. Everyone says so. Would you like me to give you lessons? The girls would all love you then!"

With the sound of Elsie's delighted laughter ringing in his ears, Arthur's face turned the colour of one of his best tomatoes before he hurried down the garden path and disappeared into the sanctuary of his potting shed.

1926

Beneath these fruit-tree boughs that shed
Their snow-white blossoms on my head,
With brightest sunshine round me spread
Of spring's unclouded weather,
In this sequestered nook how sweet
To sit upon my orchard-seat!
And birds and flowers once more to greet,
My last year's friends together.

William Wordsworth,
"The Green Linnet"

I̶N SPITE OF WOBIN'S cheery chirrup from the bough above him, Arthur sighed. How odd it felt to be sitting on the bench in his own back yard on a Monday afternoon, but on that day, 3rd May 1926, he was just one of almost two million working men across the country who had walked out on General Strike. It was the miners up north who had started it, when their bosses announced that they'd have to work longer for less pay if they wanted to keep their jobs. The trade unions called out working men everywhere in sympathy – so the buses and trains weren't running, factory machinery had ground to a halt, and the army had been called in to keep food supplies moving.

"At least those miners still have jobs," said Tom, after he'd shuffled painfully down the garden path to join Arthur. "Think how many men have already been laid off at Chatham Dockyard. But if there aren't as many ships to build, there just isn't enough work."

Arthur nodded in agreement. "Well, I've not been given my cards yet. Might come any day though."

"What was it like down there this morning?"

"Chaos. We were all gathered outside the gates. I mean, we were angry, but it was quite peaceful until the police turned up with batons. A lot of us just left then."

"Makes me glad I'm away from it now. This back of mine, it's been the ruin of me. I feel so useless."

"Oh, I don't know," smiled Arthur. "With money so tight, we've got to make this garden pay its way, and you're the expert! What do you reckon I should put where?"

"What are you thinking of planting?"

"Onions, carrots, runner beans, peas, potatoes, turnips – and I wondered about cucumbers and tomatoes? I'd like to try a few more herbs too: mint, of course, but things like sage, thyme and even dill, which Ada said was nice."

Tom's eyes narrowed as he viewed the patch. "Well, if you're planning on beans and peas, keep them away from the onions, or else they'll be stunted. Turnips don't like potatoes near them. Carrots need to be kept apart from dill, and sage is no good for cucumbers."

Arthur laughed out loud. "You see, Dad, that's why I still have so much to learn from you about gardening."

And as if he were laughing too, Wobin whistled and chirped as he swooped across to land right in front of Tom's feet, cocking his head to one side as he looked up at him. Tom dug into his pocket for some bits of meat fat that he knew Wobin loved. Stretching down to hold his hand out flat in front of the little bird, Wobin hopped onto Tom's fingers before selecting his afternoon treat, then flying away.

1927

'Tis now the summer of your youth: time has not cropped the roses from your cheek, though sorrow long has washed them.

Edward Moore, "The Gamester"

A year later, just three weeks after his twenty-first birthday, Arthur joined his brothers Dick, John and Harry as they carried their father's coffin into the church where, thirty-two years earlier, eighteen-year-old Tom had married his childhood sweetheart, Emily. As she walked behind them, supported by their married daughters Lily and Ada, Emily thought back to their long-ago wedding and how nervous she'd been as she walked down this same aisle on her father's arm. Then, Tom's smile had beamed down at her as she came towards him, filling her with confidence. She had to keep that image in her mind! Even though her eyes pricked with tears, Emily steeled herself to stare down at her best black shoes as she walked. That way, she didn't have to think about her Tom lying in the coffin in front of her. She would *not* cry, not here in front of everyone. She and Tom had never shown their feelings in public.

Arthur had made the wreath for the top of the coffin himself.

The ring of ivy had come from the cutting Tom had planted more than thirty years before, which now completely engulfed the back fence. The small white roses were from the climbing plant that Tom and his boys had dug into the garden when Ernest didn't come home from France.

The service began with Tom's favourite hymn, "Great is Thy Faithfulness", and as Arthur joined in to sing the verse he knew his father loved most, his heart lurched with an unexpected longing to believe in God again with his whole heart. He remembered how simple faith had been when he was a little boy, and his father had come to sit on his bed to hear him say his prayers.

> *Summer and winter, and springtime and harvest,*
> *Sun, moon and stars in their courses above,*
> *Join with all nature in manifold witness*
> *To thy great faithfulness, mercy and love.*

Thomas Chisholm, "Great is Thy Faithfulness"

Arthur looked up at the statue of Christ that hung above the altar, whispering under his breath as he stared at the face that had been familiar to him in this church since as long as he could remember.

"You take care of my dad, do you hear? Be faithful to him. He's a good man. He's loved you all his life. *You* have got to love him now." Arthur wiped a tear away from his cheek. "And me. If you're there, I think I could do with a bit of love too…"

Emily had wanted Tom's wake back at the house to be a low-key affair, but a surprisingly long queue of local friends made their way in to see her with heart-warming tales of times they'd spent with Tom over the years. Each one of them instructed her to knock if she needed anything, anything at all, but she knew she wouldn't. She had her family, and together they would cope, with dignity and pride, as Tom always had. Still, as each caller left the house, Emily felt warmed and cherished by the circle of neighbours who shared the ups and downs of their lives in these tightly packed terraced streets.

Emily nearly let her guard down when it was time for Dick, who was now her eldest remaining son, to return to London with Audrey, the girl he'd met through his work in the Civil Service, and married the previous year. Emily didn't cry though. No tears until later…

As the evening drew in, Emily plunged her arms into a sink of soapy water with an overwhelming sense of familiar comfort as she started to wash up the best plates and cups that had been brought out for the wake. It was John who spotted her first and insisted she should let him take over but, with the best smile she could muster, she refused his offer, thinking how handsome the twenty-two-year-old had become since he'd started at the gasworks three years earlier. Just at that moment Harry (fifteen years old, but looking every inch the young man, in spite of his frustration that it still didn't look as if he would ever grow a proper beard!) called John through to listen to the radio.

Emily's hands stilled in the water as Al Jolson's voice filled the small house. Tom always said this was *his* song, joining in with a voice that lost none of its sweetness as he grew frailer. The sound of that same song now finally broke her resolve and she let the tears fall freely into the soap suds below. And in the other room, Arthur sat down heavily in his dad's old chair to catch his breath.

When the red, red robin
Comes bob, bob, bobbin' along, along,
There'll be no more sobbin'
When he starts throbbin'
His old sweet song:
Wake up, wake up, you sleepy head
Get up, get up, get out of your bed
Cheer up, cheer up, the sun is red
Live, love, laugh and be happy!

What if I were blue –
Now I'm walkin' through
Fields of flowers.
Rain may glisten,
But still I listen
For hours and hours.
I'm just a kid again,
Doin' what I did again.
Singin' a song,
When the red, red robin
Comes bob, bob, bobbin' along.

Harry M. Woods, "When the Red, Red Robin"

And just like the kid he'd once been, Arthur dropped
his face into his hands and sobbed his heart out.

1931

See the flowers, how they grow;
Hear the winds that gently blow.
Bird and insect, flower and tree,
Know they must not idle be;
Each has something it must do –
Little children, so must you.

Rufus Merrill, "My Flower-Pot"

Arthur never minded being on babysitting duty for Ada's boys, who lived just up the road. Their dad, Albert, had struggled to find work after he'd been laid off from the road maintenance team by the council. It wasn't his fault. He was a good worker, but the Depression that followed the Wall Street Crash in America had spread its tentacles to Britain, and Albert was one of thousands of casualties across the country to lose their jobs over the past year.

"Albert's got a few hours' work putting up a garden shed today," said Ada as she dropped the boys off. "And Saturday is always my turn for helping out at the soup kitchen in town."

"Just leave them," smiled Arthur. "I hope you won't mind a bit of mud though. They'll be helping me in the garden."

Ada stooped down to kiss the boys goodbye. "I'm baking a cake for their tea. I'll drop one round for you too."

Arthur shrugged. "There won't be much of that left once Harry and Bo tuck in!"

Half an hour later, Jack, a ginger-haired six-year-old, had already got bored with gardening and was hanging over the back fence watching a lorry filling up with a load of sacks at the coal yard–even though the place was much quieter now money was tight for everyone.

Concentrating on pricking out his tomato plants, Arthur began to realize that Jack's little brother was suspiciously quiet. He turned just in time to see Freddie, cross-legged in the vegetable patch, popping a fat slug into his mouth.

"Freddie, don't! You shouldn't eat slugs!"

Chewing happily, the four-year-old turned big brown eyes towards his uncle. "Why not? I like them."

"Really? What do they taste like?"

Freddie thought for a moment before answering. "Just like worms really…"

We have descended into the garden and caught three hundred slugs. How I love the mixture of the beautiful and the squalid in gardening. It makes it so lifelike.

Evelyn Underhill, Letter to Meyrick Heath, 1912

1932

"There's a robin sitting on your spade."

When Arthur stepped out from the shed at the sound of her voice calling out from the back lane, his knees almost buckled as he took in his first vision of her: auburn curls peeping out from under her hat, her cheeks rosy from the cutting wind, and a gleam of delight in her pale green eyes. On the handle of the spade, Wobin looked from one of them to the other with interest.

"Oh, that's Wobin," said Arthur, when he finally found his voice.

"Wobin?" Those green eyes were suddenly peering at him with curiosity. "Is he a pet then?"

"No, that's just a name my little brother gave him years ago."

"Really? How old is he?"

"Oh, it's not the same Wobin," blustered Arthur. "There's a

family of them who have been here for ages, and somehow there's always one who acts like this. He's just Wobin."

The girl's response seemed to have a note of admiration in it as she asked, "Are you a bird watcher then?"

"I know all the different ones that come into the garden. I like to find where they nest too, if I can."

"Do you mean here in the garden, or do you look for birds when you're out walking too?"

"It sounds silly, I know, but I quite enjoy it."

"Not silly at all. I rather like the idea. Where do you go, to look for them?"

"Not far. Just up on the common mostly."

"Would you mind if I came with you?" For the first time, the girl seemed a little uncertain of herself.

"Well, yes, of course. When would you like to go?"

"Now?"

Arthur glanced down at his old boots and tatty trousers. "Well, I'm not really dressed for walking out…"

"You look fine to me."

"Oh," he gulped, hardly able to believe his luck. "I'm Arthur, by the way."

"Daisy, that's me," she smiled back. "Pleased to meet you!"

1933

There is a flower within my heart,
Daisy, Daisy,
Planted one day by a glancing dart,
Planted by Daisy Bell.
Whether she loves me or loves me not

Sometimes it's hard to tell;
And yet I am longing to share the lot
Of beautiful Daisy Bell.

Daisy, Daisy, give me your answer, do,
I'm half crazy all for the love of you.
It won't be a stylish marriage,
I can't afford a carriage,
But you'd look sweet upon the seat
Of a bicycle made for two.

Harry Dacre, "Daisy Bell (Bicycle Built for Two)"

Daisy didn't arrive on a bicycle, but on the back of her father's horse-drawn cart that had been covered with greenery and summer flowers especially for the occasion. Her auburn curls were scooped back under a veil onto which a ring of ferns and fresh daisies had been placed, and her simple gown of white satin was fashioned out of the wedding dress her older sister had worn the year before.

Waiting for his bride at the front of the church, Arthur thought he might faint with happiness that this wonderful girl had agreed to become his wife. As she finally reached where he stood alongside his best man Wilf, she turned round to hand her bouquet of small white roses (from her husband-to-be's garden, of course!) to her best friend Nellie, who was her only bridesmaid.

"Here we go then, Arthur!" she grinned as she took his hand.

And as they turned to start the ceremony, Arthur glanced beyond the vicar towards the figure of Christ hanging high above the altar.

"Thank you," he mouthed silently, before turning to Daisy to make his vows.

Come live with me and be my love,

And we will all the pleasures prove,

That valleys, groves, hills, and fields,

Woods, or steepy mountain yields...

And I will make thee beds of roses

And a thousand fragrant posies,

A cap of flowers, and a kirtle

Embroidered all with leaves of myrtle...

A belt of straw and ivy buds,

With coral clasps and amber studs:

And if these pleasures may thee move,

Come live with me and be my love.

Christopher Marlowe, "The Passionate Shepherd to His Love"

❧

After three days' honeymoon in Margate, the newly married couple returned to set up home in the house where Arthur had lived all his life. Emily was grateful for their company now that John had emigrated to Canada, and Harry had married Hetty, the daughter of one of his work mates at the coal company. Even her youngest, Bo, had moved into digs in Gravesend to be near his job on the barges that took cargo up and down the River Thames.

And the best thing was that Emily had liked Daisy from the moment she first met her. She approved of the young woman's forthright ways, and her willingness to roll her sleeves up and get stuck into whatever job needed to be done. She watched as Daisy played chase with the grandchildren, and licked her lips with pleasure when she discovered that Arthur's girl could cook a suet pud to match the lightness of her own. Arthur deserved that. He was a good boy, steady and loyal, and Emily had worried that love might pass this quiet, warm-hearted man by when he spent so much time happily on his own in the garden. But it was the garden that had brought Daisy to him, and Emily couldn't be more delighted.

She was, however, acutely sensitive to the needs of a newly married couple to have space and privacy, but affording a home of their own was out of the question now the household budget had dropped so dramatically as, one by one, each of her sons and daughters had moved out to get on with their lives. When Emily finally managed to discuss her feelings with Daisy, her daughter-in-law simply hugged her.

"You're not just Arthur's mum now. You're mine too. My mum died so long ago that I've forgotten what it was like to have a mother to set me on the right path. I love Arthur, and this house and garden mean so much to him. It's where he belongs. It's where you belong too. I want to join your family home, not take it over."

Emily reached over to squeeze Daisy's hand. "As long as you're sure I won't be in the way…"

"Of course not," replied Daisy emphatically. "We're just grateful you don't mind us being here. The only thing I ask is that you teach me all the things I need to know about running a home and family."

Emily laughed. "Yes, well, I have had a bit of practice at that…"

"Look at us," said the violets blooming at her feet, "all last winter we slept in the seeming death… but at the right time God awakened us, and here we are to comfort you."

Revd Edward Payson Roe, "Near to Nature's Heart"

1934

Tiptoe through the window
By the window, that is where I'll be
Come tiptoe through the tulips with me.

Oh, tiptoe from the garden
By the garden of the willow tree
And tiptoe through the tulips with me.

Knee deep in flowers we'll stray,
We'll keep the showers away
And if I kiss you in the garden, in the moonlight,
Will you pardon me?
And tiptoe through the tulips with me.

Al Dubin, "Tiptoe through the Tulips"

The following April, as the garden sparkled with bright red tulips, Daisy and Arthur became the proud parents of Alice Emily, who had her father's quiet smile combined with her mother's auburn colouring. If Arthur thought he couldn't love any more deeply than he loved his wife, this new arrival in his life stirred such passionate feelings of devotion and protection that he worried about taking his eyes off his tiny daughter, even to catch up on much-needed sleep.

Daisy, though, took to motherhood with the ease of a veteran, helped by mother-in-law Emily, who managed the delicate task of being on hand when needed, but also knew when to make a tactical withdrawal if she sensed the new parents needed to cope on their own.

What does little birdie say
In her nest at peep of day?
Let me fly, says little birdie,
Mother, let me fly away.
Birdie, rest a little longer,
Till thy little wings are stronger.
So she rests a little longer,
Then she flies away.

What does little baby say,

In her bed at peep of day?

Baby says, like little birdie,

Let me rise and fly away.

Baby, sleep a little longer,

Till thy little limbs are stronger.

If she sleeps a little longer,

Baby too shall fly away.

Lord Alfred Tennyson, "Sea Dreams"

1935

On the 8th January, in a two-room house in Tupelo, Mississippi, a couple called Vernon and Gladys were devastated when the first of their twin boys, Jessie, was stillborn. For Mr and Mrs Presley, that loss made the safe arrival of their second twin, Elvis, even more precious.

And on exactly the same day, there was great news for Arthur and the family. Elsie announced that she was getting married, which was certainly music to her mother's ears. After all, Elsie was twenty-six, and her forthright opinions about women's rights and politics could sometimes make her uncomfortable company. She'd never gone along with the accepted view that women belonged in the home and were good for little else. Quickly bored with her first job as a typist in the office of "Samuel Morrison, Solicitor", she spent long months studying at home and night school to learn the new skill of Pitman's New Era shorthand. The moment she was able to take down dictation at 100 words a minute, she informed Mr Morrison that if he didn't promote her to secretary, and give her a pay rise to match her new status, she would be taking her exceptional skills elsewhere. Admiring her spirit, but wondering how much trouble it might bring him in the future, Mr Morrison decided to give her a chance.

Within three months, she was organizing his life as efficiently in the office as his wife did at home. Elsie was nothing less than a treasure – which was exactly what his son, Samuel Morrison Junior, thought when he joined the family business three years later, having completed his law studies. He liked the spiky young woman who could spot errors in a legal document a mile off, and argue her case if he didn't immediately agree with her. She was often right, though, and young Samuel found he valued her contribution more and more as they settled into an easy working partnership.

It took him six months to pluck up the courage to ask her to the pictures, because honestly he thought she might turn him down flat. But she said Yes – and when he reached out to clasp her hand in the dark and she didn't pull back, he knew he never wanted to let her go.

Their wedding in August was a very grand affair, befitting the status of Morrison and Son, Solicitors, in the local area. The happy couple settled into their brand new house on a prestigious estate on the outskirts of town, and when Sam invested £100 in one of the brand new Morris Minors, Elsie learned to drive immediately.

On the day before Christmas Eve, a delivery van arrived with a present for Emily, Arthur and Daisy. It was a refrigerator – the new kitchen appliance that Elsie now felt no home should be without. Emily smiled at the thought of all the years she'd managed perfectly well in the past, but as their milk and eggs chilled, her heart warmed to the benefits of having such a well-to-do and loving daughter.

1936

What do we look for as reward?
Some little sounds, and scents, and scenes:
A small hand darting strawberry-ward
A woman's aprons full of greens...

The sense that we have brought to birth
Out of the cold and heavy soil,
These blessed fruits and flowers of earth
Is large reward for all our toil.

Ruth Pitter, "The Diehards"

THE YEAR 1936 started with the sad news of the death of the popular King George V, which meant that his eldest son, Edward, succeeded to the throne. Within months, whispers were circulating that Edward was planning to marry an American woman, Wallis Simpson, who had divorced her first husband and was in the process of divorcing her second. Edward's final decision was to abdicate the throne in order to marry "the woman I love". His mother, Queen Mary, was overheard acidly commenting in disbelief that Edward should "give up all this for that", before her second son, Albert, the personal choice of King George to follow him onto the throne, was crowned under his chosen name, King George VI.

The saga of the Royals was the fascinating subject of chatter in pubs, on doorsteps and over garden fences the length and breadth of the country.

"That Edward's got the right idea, if you ask me," said Wilf from his side of the fence, reaching over to the tin plate Daisy had balanced on the gatepost between the two gardens to try a piece of the bread pudding she had made earlier that morning from a stale loaf, spices and dried fruit all soaked in milk, then baked in the oven. Daisy, who was at the end of the garden shaking the apple tree so that some of the biggest cookers fell straight into her apron skirt, plainly didn't approve of Wilf's comment supporting the behaviour of the lovelorn king.

"Wilf Green, you are certainly no gentleman – and neither is that Edward. All those privileges he's had, and he hasn't got the gumption to do his duty. Ordinary men like Arthur's brother Ernest laid down their lives for England. And Edward couldn't even give up a floozy who'd already seen off two husbands!"

"It's romantic," retorted Wilf, his eyes sparkling with mischief. "I thought you women liked the idea of a man giving up everything for love of a fair maiden."

"Well, you've had your fair share of loving fair maidens," countered Daisy. "Are you ever going to settle down, Wilf?"

Wilf shrugged. "Probably not."

"Your poor mum must despair of you!"

"Nope, not at all," replied Wilf, "and she's all the woman I need. No girl is ever going to mean more to me than my mum."

"You could maybe help your mum out a little more, Wilf," ventured Arthur as he walked up to join the conversation. "How about giving her a hand in the garden? It's full of weeds, and she can't manage it alone."

"I'll have you know that the garden is exactly how she likes it," said Wilf, his face a picture of guileless innocence. "She's always favoured the natural look. She says that if buttercups and dandelions are good enough for the countryside, they're good enough for her."

"You're making that up," said Daisy, her lips twitching with laughter.

"Am I?"

And when Daisy caught sight of the wink Wilf aimed at Arthur, she grabbed a cooking apple from her apron and lobbed it smartly in Wilf's direction.

A poor old Widow in her weeds
Sowed her garden with wild-flower seeds;
Not too shallow, and not too deep,
And down came April – drip – drip – drip.
Up shone May, like gold, and soon
Green as an arbour grew leafy June.
And now all summer she sits and sews
Where willow herb, comfrey, bugloss blows,
Teasle and pansy, meadowsweet,
Campion, toadflax, and rough hawksbit;
Brown bee orchis, and Peals of Bells;
Clover, burnet, and thyme she smells;
Like Oberon's meadows her garden is
Drowsy from dawn to dusk with bees.

Weeps she never, but sometimes sighs,
And peeps at her garden with bright brown eyes;
And all she has is all she needs –
A poor Old Widow in her weeds.

Walter de la Mare, "A Widow's Weeds"

1937

Given half a chance, three-year-old Alice would follow her cousins, Jack and Freddie, anywhere. Arthur watched from the back room window as his daughter plodded round the garden after them like a shadow. Now aged ten, Freddie had given up eating slugs, and his burning interest instead was to try and collect more sticky-backed cigarette cards for his album than his big brother Jack, who, like almost every other twelve-year-old, took the hobby very seriously. Anyone who smoked Wills or Players cigarettes was a target, because each cigarette packet might contain a card from collections of famous cricketers, footballers or film stars. Freddie was especially proud of one precious card given to *him* (not Jack!) by his Auntie Elsie. It celebrated the Coronation of King George VI in May earlier that year – and Jack was green with envy!

"So what!" announced Jack. "Auntie Elsie gave me this!" Triumphantly he held his hand high in the air, clutching the very first copy of a new comic called *The Dandy*.

"Don't care," snorted Freddie, who really did care very much. "That comic will never catch on. Cartoons are boring!"

"Oh," said Jack, pointedly looking through the pages of the comic, "you won't want to come on our trip to the Regal cinema to see *Snow White and the Seven Dwarfs* when it comes out then?"

"I do! Auntie Elsie said I could come."

"But you don't like cartoons!"

"I like *some* cartoons," protested Freddie, but Jack had already got up and, with a superior huff, walked away.

Watching from the side, little Alice had no idea why Freddie was upset, but she knew hugs helped – so she wrapped her chubby little arms around her favourite cousin, and planted a wet kiss on his cheek.

The innocence of their chatter caused Arthur to shudder a little as he watched. They couldn't know how worrying the news was every day now – about Herr Hitler and his plans for the German people to have more "living space". These were worrying times.

So Arthur did then what he always did when he wanted to put bad thoughts out of his mind. He put on his boots and headed for the garden. He could bury a lot of troubles digging in the dirt.

How fair is a garden amid the trials and passions
of existence.

Benjamin Disraeli

1938

In July 1938, on the day it was announced that Howard Hughes had managed to fly around the world in just ninety hours, Daisy also found out that she was expecting a new addition to their family. During the weeks that followed, Arthur found himself wondering at the wisdom of bringing a new life into such an unsettled world. At the yard, it had been clear for some time that increasing amounts of money were being allocated to rearming and the defence of the British nation as Germany became more aggressive. And when, in September that year, Prime Minister Neville Chamberlain returned from meeting Adolf Hitler and spoke on the radio of "peace in our time", Arthur felt a shiver of dread slide down his spine.

1939

As daffodils trumpeted gloriously across the garden, Daisy gave birth to a baby boy they called Thomas Ernest. And six months later, on 1st September 1939, after the Nazis had invaded Poland, Britain declared war on Germany.

1940

At Chatham Dockyard, work was hard and long for the huge workforce that was taken on to build and repair submarines and warships, as the country readied itself for the German onslaught. Hitler considered Britain's great weakness was that it was an island, so he started by torpedoing merchant ships bringing supplies to its shores in a relentless U-boat campaign. If he thought he could starve "Old Blighty" that way, Hitler didn't know much about the British Bulldog spirit that had men like Arthur, already exhausted from endless hours at the yard, immediately heading for the garden, which he was turning into a kitchen larder for all the neighbours. He dug up the flowerbeds, filled in the pond, and even smashed up the garden path so that every inch of soil could be used to grow vegetables.

He remembered his father's advice about what vegetables would flourish best alongside others, but in the end he decided that this was no time for niceties. With grim determination, he set about digging in potatoes, turnips, carrots and onions, the basic fare to fill stomachs. And if thoughts of impending invasion crept into his mind, he found himself recalling St Francis of Assisi's response to a question he was asked:

> "What would you do if you were suddenly to learn that you were to die at sunset today?" He replied, "I would finish hoeing my garden."

In kitchens up and down the street, Arthur's produce was added to whatever butter, bacon, egg powder and sugar their neighbours' ration cards would allow, along with the occasional treat of a real egg or orange. Pies and stews were shared among families, especially if anyone could come up with a chicken – or even a rabbit or two, like the ones immortalized in the wartime favourite recorded by Flanagan and Allen, who got the whole country singing.

Every man between the ages of eighteen and forty-one was called up, apart from those who worked in "reserved occupations", like Arthur and all the thousands of men now conscripted into the dockyard. Men working in utilities were needed at home too –

but twenty-nine-year-old Harry, broad-shouldered and strong from years of delivering coal, which was one of the vital jobs providing exemption from having to sign up, ignored the pleas of his wife Hetty, and joined the army straight away. Bo, the youngest brother, also left his cargo job on the River Thames, and headed to the recruitment office along with Harry.

Emily stood stoically at the garden gate as she watched her two youngest boys walk up the street and out of sight on their way to war, just as she had watched Ernest back in 1916. And the moment she was behind closed doors, she sank to her knees and buried her head in her hands.

"Oh God, bring my boys home. Dear *God*, bring them home…"

Our England is a garden, and such gardens are not made
By singing: "Oh, how beautiful," and sitting in the shade…

Rudyard Kipling,
"The Glory of the Garden"

At first, there were months when the country held its breath and wondered whether this war was really going to affect them much at home. Then, when the Nazis swept across France on the same day in May 1940 that Winston Churchill became prime minister, the need for Britain to battle for its life was clear. On the 4th June, families everywhere huddled round their radios to hear Churchill declare:

> *Whatever the cost may be, we shall fight on the beaches, we shall fight on the landing grounds, we shall fight in the fields and in the streets, we shall fight in the hills; we shall never surrender.*

For just over three months, the Battle of Britain raged in the skies over Kent. Across the Medway towns, terrified yet fascinated neighbours stood out in their gardens, cheering on the British Hurricanes and the plucky little Spitfires as they swooped across the skies in dogfights with the German Messerschmitts.

One morning, while Emily was keeping an eye on her grandchildren Tommy and Alice indoors, Daisy stood rooted to the ground by the back fence, unable to tear her eyes away from the scene above her. A Spitfire had scored a hit on a Messerschmitt, and she watched as the German pilot bailed out to parachute to the ground. She was near enough to see how young he was, and the terror on his face as the Spitfire turned back to circle around him, strafing him as he fell. He landed in the coal depot behind the house, just yards from where Daisy stood. Bile rose in her throat as she staggered back inside, slamming the kitchen door behind her, and pulling a startled Tommy into her arms. That pilot had been the enemy – that was true – but he was also some mother's son, and for that woman and the grief coming her way, Daisy hugged her baby tightly and wept.

1942

When lilacs last in the dooryard bloom'd,
And the great star early droop'd in the western sky in the night,
I mourn'd, and yet shall mourn with ever-returning spring.

Ever-returning spring, trinity sure to me you bring,
Lilac blooming perennial and drooping star in the west,
And thought of him I love...

Over the breast of the spring, the land, amid cities,
Amid lanes and through old woods, where lately the violets
peep'd from the ground, spotting the gray debris,
Amid the grass in the fields each side of the lanes,
passing the endless grass,
Passing the yellow-spear'd wheat, every grain from its shroud in
the dark-brown fields uprisen,
Passing the apple-tree blows of white and pink in the orchards,
Carrying a corpse to where it shall rest in the grave,
Night and day journeys a coffin...

Walt Whitman,
"When Lilacs Last in the Dooryard Bloom'd"

As years of war rolled on, "normal" life was not very normal at all. Everyone, even those children who'd been sent to the countryside as evacuees, had to carry gas masks. Six-year-old Alice came home from school giggling at how all the boys had lined up to have a pudding basin put on their head so that any protruding hair could be snipped off to make sure their gas masks were a snug fit. The pavements were pitch-black at night when street lights were switched off, and families put up black-out curtains and sticky brown tape over every window. New clothes were a thing of the past, and children got used to hand-me-downs that may have been worn by several older siblings before reaching them.

While Arthur's garden was covered with rows of growing vegetables, others had dug deep for glory, creating air-raid shelters stacked with tinned food and makeshift beds where families and neighbours could weather the storm during yet another night of bombing. Bread and dripping became everyone's regular breakfast and often dinner too, and among the rubble of bombed buildings, boys had fun tying ropes to lamp posts, then taking off and swinging round with their feet off the ground. Meanwhile, girls played hopscotch or strung lines across the street for skipping, chanting rhymes as they jumped.

My young man has gone to France,
To teach the ladies how to dance.
When he comes back,
He'll marry me,
And we'll dance the polka 1 2 3
1 2 3, 1 2 3,

We'll dance the polka 1 2 3.

Now that many of the regular postmen were away at war, teenage boys on bikes were co-opted to deliver longed-for letters from the men overseas. And all too often they made the most dreaded delivery of all: a telegram bearing the heart-breaking news that a treasured son or devoted dad had died in action. Each morning, along with every other woman in the street, Emily flicked back the curtains with a sense of dread at the sound of a bike coming up the street. When that bike finally stopped at their door with a telegram, Emily took the envelope with shaking hands, then put it straight into her apron pocket. She had been dreading this. She could guess the contents. If she didn't open it, the reality of what had happened and who she'd lost could wait a while.

When Arthur returned from his dockyard shift several hours later, he found his mother sitting in the upright armchair that his father

Tom had always loved. Her body was rigid with tension, her eyes unseeing as she stared ahead of her. Arthur looked down to see the small brown envelope clutched tightly in her hands. He knelt down and slowly pulled the envelope out of her stiff fingers. Seconds later, he slumped back on his haunches as he read the words "missing, presumed dead". It was Bo, the baby of the boys, last heard from months earlier when he had got word to them explaining that his regiment had been assigned to a place that was very far away. He had sounded so excited.Much later, they had realized from the shocking news headlines that he was probably in the Far East, where the Allied boys were experiencing terrible treatment at the hands of the Japanese. And now this. Bo wouldn't be coming home. Emily's tears started to fall then, and Arthur scooped his mother into his arms, his body wracked with choking sobs as he held her.

As similar envelopes arrived at the homes of so many around them, neighbours became friends, and friends became family, uniting their community in shared grief and dogged determination. And although tears were never far away, laughter was close too. Emily even managed a smile herself a few days later when she was in the garden watching Alice and Tommy wandering hand in hand through Arthur's vegetable patch.

"And *this* is the cabbage patch," explained Alice in her best schoolma'am tones to her bemused little brother. "Mummy says cabbage patches are important because big birds called storks bring babies there. They fly with a square towel in their beaks carrying the new baby, then leave it in the cabbage patch in your back yard. But Mummy says there aren't many babies at the moment because those German Nasties have been shooting down the storks so they can't bring any more."

May we be good to plants and flowers. May we take fine care of the places where they grow. Earth won't have to shake and flood and burn so fiercely then. The world will be more wide-awake and tuneful, a place where children – all beings – can bloom.

Maggie Steincrohn Davis, from Glory! To the Flowers

1944

"Careless talk costs lives!"

That was the urgent wartime message on notices posted everywhere: at work, in the streets, shops and pubs.

For a nation where neighbours had always gossiped over their garden fences, it took a while to get used to the idea that there could be German sympathizers everywhere, and that idle chit-chat about whatever wartime work you were involved in might bring danger to others. But with a huge naval dockyard like Chatham in the heart of their community, no one in this corner of Kent needed to be told that something big was coming. By 1944, nearly 1,400 ships had been repaired or refitted at the yard during the war years, but this new build-up was unprecedented.

By June of that year, more than 160,000 Allied troops had gathered along the southern coast of England. On the night of the 6th June, Operation Overlord, the largest naval, land and air operation in history, targeted the beaches of Normandy, with 18,000 paratroopers first dropping into the invasion zone, preparing the way for a fleet of 7,000 naval battleships, destroyers, minesweepers and landing craft to deposit 132,000 ground troops onto the beaches. The D-Day campaign to liberate north-west Europe from German occupation was underway!

Less than a year later, on the 7th May 1945, Germany surrendered to the Allies – and the following day people danced in the streets as "Victory in Europe" parties were held right across Britain. Daisy joined all the mums in their road to organize the most joyful party anyone could ever remember. There were cakes, biscuits, jelly and custard, and people who had never met before hugged and kissed each other with tears of relief shining in their eyes.

Looking at the tea tables lined up either side of the street, draped in garlands and flags and surrounded by excited children, Emily suddenly felt very old. In her seventy-four years, she had lived through two world wars. She had seen three sons march off to war, and none of them had returned. There was no further news of Bo following the telegram, and although they'd heard that Harry was on his way home, who knew when he would arrive, or what state he'd be in? Suddenly overwhelmed with memories of her beloved Tom, she made her way through the house towards the garden he had loved so well. It was no surprise to find Arthur there, sitting on the bench as he looked across the functional lines of vegetables that had replaced the flowers and shrubs Tom had lovingly planted.

They sat together in silence, their hands entwined, when a movement further down the garden caught their attention. The only bush Arthur had not dug out was the precious white rose Tom had planted after Ernest had died. The first white buds were appearing amid its bright green foliage – and there, on the branch nearest them, was Wobin, an old friend neither of them had seen since the start of the war.

With tears in his eyes, Arthur turned to his mother and drew her into his arms. "We've done it, Mum," he whispered. "We've got through it. We're done with this now."

Keep a green tree in your heart and perhaps a
singing bird will come.

Chinese proverb

On the day he came home, Emily heard his familiar whistle long before she saw him. Harry had always been the strongest of her boys, and yet the man who strode towards her now had a weariness etched into his face that had aged him far beyond his years.

Seeing her at the gate, he broke into a run and scooped her up into his arms, holding her so tight she could hardly breathe.

"Did you hear, Mum?" he exclaimed, stretching out his arms so that he could see her properly. "Bo is alive! They got a message through to me at the barracks. The Japanese captured him in Singapore and he's been a prisoner-of-war ever since, but they're shipping him back now. He's coming home, Mum. We're all coming home!"

1946

When you have only two pennies left in the world,
buy a loaf of bread with one,
and a lily with the other.

Chinese proverb

$\mathscr{A}$FTER ALL THE years of austerity and fear, there was optimism in the air as communities everywhere started to clear up and rebuild their broken towns and streets. On the outskirts of town, the council had erected what the locals called "Tin City" for families who'd lost their houses when wartime bombs rained down on them, destroying not just homes but lives too. As the prefabricated dwellings rose in record time, so did the gossip about them.

"They won't last ten minutes," scoffed George, Arthur's supervisor in the carpentry department at the yard. "No craftsmanship in those things. One blast of a cold Kent wind and they'll be halfway up the Medway and out to sea!"

But over the garden gates down their street, the women were eyeing the new arrivals very differently.

"Bathrooms in the house! That's what my friend Bob told us, and he should know because he's one of the builders. And those prefabs have got a toilet indoors!"

That news was greeted in stunned silence by all these women who had grown up never knowing anything other than visits to the outside privy next to the coal hole in the garden. No one ever took more time than was absolutely necessary for the simple reason that "the smallest room" was freezing cold in the winter and full of spiders for the rest of the year. It was beyond their wildest dreams to be able to have a bath in the house that wasn't in an old tin tub that you had to get down from its hook on the scullery wall – a bath that was *plumbed in* too!

"I'd have one," sighed Mary, who ran the local corner shop with her husband.

So would I! thought Daisy, sharing the feelings of every woman in the street.

Choosing her moment carefully, Daisy brought up the subject of the prefabs and their modern conveniences when the family were around the table tucking into their meal of pease pudding and ham later that day.

"It would be nice to have a toilet in the house, wouldn't it?" she suggested.

"Not a priority though," said Arthur, reaching out for another piece of bread and butter. "We've managed perfectly well for years."

"And fancy having a bath that's plumbed in!" mused Daisy, not taking her eyes off her dinner plate so that her comment sounded off-hand and casual. She had been married to Arthur for too many years to underestimate how important it was for him, as the head of the household, to be the one to come up with all the significant ideas and plans for his family.

Arthur didn't answer, perhaps because he had a mouthful of

ham hock, or perhaps because he simply didn't want to. Glancing towards her daughter-in-law, Emily restarted the conversation.

"Well, I must say I never thought I'd see things like that. I've had thirteen babies. What I would have given for hot water coming out of a tap into a bath I didn't have to lug off the wall! Whatever next?"

"Well, there's a lot we've got to sort out in this house first," said Arthur firmly. "And that means being careful with our money. Mind you…" he added, smiling towards Daisy, "I think you could do with a new cooker."

"Really?" cried Daisy, her eyes shining. "Elsie's got one of those New World cookers that are in the Gas Board showroom window." With a cheeky expression on her face, she reached out to touch Arthur's hand. "I could make you some wonderful meals on a cooker like that!"

He grinned. "Okay, we'll take a look."

"Auntie Elsie and Uncle Sam have got a television set," interrupted Alice who, at twelve years old, was becoming the image of her auburn-haired mother. "Can we get one?"

"No," was Arthur's instant reply. "They're nothing more than a gimmick and far too expensive."

"Oh, Dad!" wailed Tommy. "They've got cowboy films on them."

"You can see cowboy films at the Regal Kids' Club on a Saturday morning. We don't need a television for that. Besides, I've got to sort the garden out too. How do you all fancy helping me build a proper greenhouse next to the shed?"

"Lovely idea, dear," replied Daisy smoothly when silence descended around the table. "More gravy?"

I want to grow something.
It seems impossible that desire
can sometimes transform into devotion;
but this has happened.
And that is how I've survived:
how the hole I carefully tended
in the garden of my heart
grew a heart to fill it.

Alice Walker, "Desire"

No one in the family volunteered to help Arthur with the greenhouse, except Tommy, who showed an interest for about ten minutes before he wandered off, having realized that his dad wasn't going to let him have a hammer or saw, and anything less was completely boring. Honestly, Arthur didn't mind. This was *his* garden, handed down from father to son. Perhaps in time his own son would find the same fascination in the miracle of growing things that he'd always had, but Tommy was only seven years old, and Arthur was wise enough to know he had to discover that wonder and fascination when he was good and ready.

Building the structure was a welcome relief in some ways from the back-breaking work he'd put into digging out the vegetable patch that had claimed every inch of the back yard during the war years and every spare moment of his time ever since. At first, Arthur had thought he would just reshape the garden exactly as it had been during his father's day, but then he started to consider some of the new ideas in gardening circles, and decided that he would try to create something of his own that combined modern techniques with more traditional approaches. The greenhouse was all part of that. He could already imagine how it would look, with its shelves of home-nurtured bedding plants like geraniums, pelargoniums and petunias. He'd even considered whether he could aim for the local flower show with his attempts at huge gladioli stems or chrysanthemums the size of tea plates – and just imagine how spectacular his cucumbers might be if they were grown in a *proper* greenhouse instead of the battered, draughty old lean-to his father Tom had put up decades ago.

Arthur straightened his aching back for a moment, glancing up and down the row of terraced gardens to either side of him as he wiped his handkerchief across his hot face. There was Wilf's garden next door that, once again, was knee-high in long grass ever since Arthur had stopped using it to grow vegetables after the war. Beyond that lay a motley selection of back yards, some with small lawns surrounded by rose bushes, others just simple concrete on which he could see a selection of prams, bikes and discarded toys. No one on this side of the street had a greenhouse, he thought with pride. Just wait until the neighbours saw what he could achieve with such a splendid new addition to his little corner of England!

But there were no shortcuts. Foundations had to be dug, walls built, and a framework erected to hold the glass panes secure. Arthur stuffed the hankie back in his pocket, picked up the spade and got to work.

What a man needs in gardening is a cast-iron back
with a hinge in it.

Charles Dudley Warner, from My Summer in a Garden

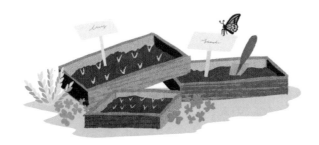

1948

Oh, Adam was a gardener, and God who made him sees
That half a proper gardener's work is done upon his knees,
So when your work is finished, you can wash
your hands and pray
For the Glory of the Garden, that it may not pass away!

Rudyard Kipling, "The Glory of the Garden"

Daisy clasped her Arthur's hand tightly as the vicar announced the winner of the Best Chrysanthemum in the church flower show of 1948. As the rather formidable chairwoman of the local Ladies' Flower Guild stood up to claim her prize, Daisy caught the disappointment in Arthur's eyes.

"Ne'er mind," he said at once. "Look, there's Bo!"

As Bo strolled across to them now, an image shot into Arthur's mind of his youngest brother as he'd looked when he'd first come back from the war. Then, he'd been just a shadow of the young man who'd marched off to join up in 1939. Those years as a Japanese prisoner-of-war had aged him, leaving silver strands in his hair and dark circles under his eyes that had stayed with him ever since. Worst of all for those who loved him were the memories that had haunted him ever since, as images of what he'd seen and been through woke him in cold sweats after yet another nightmare. He had been offered his old job again on the Thames barges, but he turned it down because he felt an overwhelming need to be at home, surrounded by familiar people and places. Emily made it her mission to ensure life was as gentle as possible for her sensitive, troubled son, and slowly, very slowly, the wounds of both his body and mind began to heal.

But by far the best medicine for Bo turned out to be something quite beyond Emily's control. Holding Bo's hand as they walked to join Arthur's family that day at the flower show was Dora, the wife who'd been giving him strength, encouragement and unconditional love since the couple married the previous year. Her first husband, Jack, had been killed on the Normandy beaches on D-Day, leaving her with twin daughters to bring up alone. Rosemary and Christine had been too young to remember their own father before he left for war, so they happily accepted that Bo was their new dad, creating together a contented and close family unit. The twins were even more delighted to know that Bo and Dora were expecting a new arrival for their family in January the following year, which was very exciting news. Now nine years old, the girls bounded over to hug their auntie and uncle.

"Are Alice and Tommy here, Auntie Daisy?"

"I gave them tuppence each for the sweet stall over there at the back of the hall. I bet Tommy has bought a bag of gobstoppers!"

Arthur laughed. "And dolly mixtures for Alice, I reckon!"

"Probably," laughed Daisy. "Shall we all go and see?"

Alice ran to greet her cousins when she saw the family group making their way down the hall.

"Look! These are called parma violets, and they taste just like perfume."

"Euck!" commented Tommy, sticking out his tongue. "Look at these black Jack chews. My tongue's turned black!"

"What, no gobstoppers?" asked Daisy with surprise.

Arthur had moved over to the stall to take a closer look. Spotting a big slab of toffee, which was his favourite, he handed it to the man behind the stall, who took out a small hammer so that he could break the toffee slab into bite-sized pieces before popping them all into a white paper bag.

"And you, Mummy?" asked Tommy between chews. "What are you going to choose?"

Daisy took her time gazing at the sherbet lemons, liquorice allsorts and coconut ice, all of which she liked, but finally she pointed to a jar of small, brightly coloured gums.

"Floral gums," remarked Arthur. "How appropriate for a lovely lady named after the sweetest and most humble of flowers."

With little here to do or see
Of things that in the great world be,
Sweet Daisy! oft I talk to thee
For thou art worthy,
Thou unassuming commonplace
Of Nature, with that homely face,
And yet with something of a grace
Which love makes for thee!

Bright flower! whose home is everywhere
Bold in maternal Nature's care
And all the long year through the heir
Of joy or sorrow,
Methinks that there abides in thee
Some concord with humanity,
Given to no other flower I see
The forest through.

William Wordsworth, "To the Daisy" and "To the Same Flower"

1951

The rabbit has a charming face:
Its private life is a disgrace.
I really dare not name to you
The awful things that rabbits do;
Things that your paper never prints –
You only mention them in hints.
They have such lost, degraded souls
No wonder they inhabit holes;
When such depravity is found
It only can live underground.

Author unknown, "The Rabbit"

Arthur wouldn't have minded if those darned rabbits would *stay* underground, but whenever he pulled back the curtain as he set off for work before seven each weekday morning, he saw an army of them, all enjoying a leisurely breakfast courtesy of his lettuces, not to mention the brightly coloured shoots of his gazanias, marigolds and pansies. He'd tried every remedy he could lay his hands on. Rabbits were supposed to turn their noses up at rhubarb and leeks, but they'd happily munched through the lot when he tried planting them between the beans they loved best of all. He'd hung shiny cooking pots at the end of the rows, until Daisy complained that she couldn't cook a meal for the family with just the two saucepans he'd left hanging up on the kitchen wall. He'd even borrowed Harry's dog for a day or two, but that boxer turned out to be completely soppy and terrified of any rabbit he saw!

So the battle continued, and the rabbits were winning paws down, until the wonderful day when Wilf arrived at the door with a big green-eyed furball of a cat who apparently was a stray that'd kept appearing at Handy Andy's, the ironmonger's and haberdasher's shop in the high street where Wilf had finally got a job.

"No one has laid claim to him even though we've put up lots of notices," explained Wilf, "and he's such a lovely fella. We've called him Sparky because the first time we saw him, he'd made himself at home in our electrical spares cupboard. I wondered if your youngsters might like him?"

Alice was reaching for the cat in an instant. "Sparky, like 'Sparky and the Magic Piano!'" she exclaimed, burying her head in the cat's long fur. "That's my favourite piece of music on *Children's Hour* when Uncle Mac plays it on Saturday morning radio. We've got to keep him. Tommy will love him!"

Arthur thought the whole thing was a terrible idea, but once Tommy had declared that Sparky was *definitely* going to sleep on *his* bed, he gave up trying to argue. It wasn't until a few weeks later when he pulled back the bedroom curtains to see Sparky sitting firmly in the middle of the garden path, with Wobin perched on the fence alongside looking on with interest – and not a rabbit in sight – that he made a promise to himself that Sparky would be getting extra rations of meat scraps from now on!

Two weeks later, Sparky gave birth to three kittens. *He* had obviously met up with more than just electrical sockets in Wilf's cupboard. Daisy took her to the vet's, found homes for the kittens – and Sparky was a much-loved member of the family for many years to come.

> *Two little bunnies, bless their souls,*
> *Go into hiding in their holes,*
> *And they emerge a seething mob,*
> *It must have been an inside job.*

Author unknown

The things which I have here before promised,
I will perform and keep. So help me God. Throughout all
my life and with all my heart I shall strive to be worthy of
your trust.

Her Majesty Queen Elizabeth II at her coronation

The weeks leading up to the Coronation of their beautiful young Queen Elizabeth had the country in a frenzy, and Arthur's street was no exception. Everyone caught the Coronation bug as buntings were strung up, flags hung from upstairs windows and crisp white sheets freshly laundered for the row of tea tables to be lined up along the street. Children and husbands were shooed out of kitchens in every home as mums prepared platefuls of sandwiches filled with spam and piccalilli, cheese and salad cream, or egg and cress, and cakes of all sizes were lovingly iced and adorned with shining balls or bright cherries – anything as long as it was red, white and blue. There were wobbly jellies, jugs full of strawberry squash, and obligatory Union Jack hats, not just for the children but the grown-ups too.

If that wasn't enough, in Arthur's household there was even greater cause for excitement. Their very first television set arrived just before the big day, and they'd all crowded into the front parlour to hear the Radio Rentals man explain how it worked. Thirteen-year-old Tommy asked the most questions, so from then on he was acknowledged as the expert in the family who understood the complexities of this mysterious new contraption better than anyone else.

The room was packed to the rafters the following day as they all peered at the tiny black and white screen to see the procession of grand carriages taking the royal party along the streets of London towards Westminster Abbey, followed by the magical sight of the Queen making her stately way down the aisle to begin the ceremony.

"Her dress is just heavenly," sighed Alice who, at nineteen, considered herself an expert on modern fashions. "It's all white silk, and the embroidery has taken months."

"Did you know," said Arthur, glasses perched on his nose as he read from the newspaper he had balanced on his knee, "that the dress is embroidered with flower emblems from all the countries of the Commonwealth? The Tudor rose of England, the Scottish thistle, the Welsh leek, the wattle of Australia, the maple leaf of Canada, the New Zealand fern, that great big coloured flower, the protea, from South Africa, two lotus flowers from India and Ceylon, and wheat, cotton and jute from Pakistan. And for luck, there's an Irish shamrock – *and* a four-leaf clover embroidered just where the Queen's hand will touch it throughout the day."

"That's boring!" retorted Alice. "Keep quiet, Dad – we can't hear what the commentator is saying!"

With a smile, Daisy laid her hand over Arthur's and gave it a squeeze. Smiling back, he leaned across to whisper in her ear, "Daisies are *my* favourite flower…"

And later, after neighbours young and old had had their fill of party tea, there was dancing in the street as everyone grabbed partners and twirled around to "Coronation Rag" by pianist Winifred Atwell, "Side by Side" by Kay Starr and "In a Golden Coach, there's a Heart of Gold" by Billy Cotton and his team from *The Band Show*, which was a highlight every week on the BBC's Light Programme. And after the smaller children had giggled and wiggled their way through Guy Mitchell's "She Wears Red Feathers" before winding down as Frankie Laine sang "Tell me a Story", Arthur swung Daisy into his arms for the song that reminded him of that specially positioned little plant embroidered on the new Queen's Coronation gown.

1954

O Christmas tree, O Christmas tree,
Thy leaves are so unchanging!
O Christmas tree, O Christmas tree,
Thy leaves are so unchanging!

Not only green when summer's here,
But also when it's cold and drear.
O Christmas tree, O Christmas tree,
Thy leaves are so unchanging!

Ernst Anschütz / German folk song, "O Tannenbaum"

Ever since the war, when Arthur had bought a tiny fir tree in a pot that they had decorated with shiny baubles for that first peaceful Christmas in 1945, he'd got into the habit of planting the same tree back into a corner of the garden, so that he could bring it inside again the following year. By 1954, the tree was almost touching the parlour ceiling, and it took him and Tommy, who was already very tall for a fifteen-year-old, quite a while to wedge it in between the sideboard and the television set. Alice, who was constantly reminding anyone who'd listen that she would be twenty-one the following year, so *nobody* could tell her what to do, took charge of the decorations. There were delicate glass ornaments, silver tinsel that looked like icicles, candles and holders that clipped onto the ends of branches, and satin ribbon bows of red and gold. Stretched across the walls were rows of Christmas cards from well-wishers, and Alice made Tommy help her for a whole evening as they licked and stuck together brightly coloured paper chains long enough to be strung across the ceiling from every corner of the room.

On Christmas morning, Arthur gently guided Emily, who was surprisingly sprightly for an eighty-three-year-old, into the high-backed chair in the corner of the back room so that she had a good view as the family opened the pile of festively wrapped presents under the tree. Bo and Dora's twin daughters Christine and Rosemary were the first to open their identical boxes containing roller skates, which were all the rage with teenagers. Their little brother David loved his Sooty Songster Xylophone, and Ada's granddaughter Florence, who was the same age as David, squealed with delight when she saw her Rosebud dolly, with golden curls and cherry-red lips, who gave a pitiful cry when she was turned upside down. With a shout of triumph, Tommy unwrapped his green and red Meccano set packed full of metal strips, plates, girders, wheels, pulleys and gears, and immediately disappeared upstairs to find a quiet corner to start work on his construction.

Just as Arthur held up the dark brown sleeveless pullover knitted for him by his sister Ada, Daisy opened his present to her: a sturdy leather handbag that was just what she needed.

"And this one's for you, Gran," said Daisy, handing Emily a red parcel topped with a silver bow. Emily unwrapped it carefully, folding the paper neatly so that she could save it for next year.

"This is lovely, Daisy," she said, as she pulled out a soft grey wool shawl, which she put up to her cheek to feel its softness. "You've done beautiful crochet work on this. Thank you."

After that, Emily sat back in her chair and gazed around at all her family members who were packed into the room. How Tom would have loved to see this – to take pride in all that his sons and daughters had achieved, the partners they'd chosen, and the grandchildren they'd brought into the world to add to the family clan.

And what a different world it was since she and Tom had set out on their married life all those years ago. Her brow furrowed as she tried to remember just when that was: 1895? Was that it? Was it really nearly sixty-five years ago that they had walked down the aisle?

And as images slid through her mind, of babies she'd nursed, sons she'd seen march off to war, tears she'd shed, neighbours she'd loved and lost, times of contentment, laughter and joy, she closed her eyes amid all the bustle of family Christmas, and nodded off to sleep.

O Christmas tree, O Christmas tree,
You'll ever be unchanging!
A symbol of goodwill and love,
You'll ever be unchanging!

Each shining light, each silver bell,
No one alive spreads cheer so well.
O Christmas tree, O Christmas tree,
You'll ever be unchanging!

1956

Look out! Look out! Jack Frost is about!
He's after our fingers and toes;
And all through the night, the gay little sprite
Is working where nobody knows.

He'll climb each tree, so nimble is he,
His silvery powder he'll shake.
To windows he'll creep and while we're asleep
Such wonderful pictures he'll make.

Across the grass he'll merrily pass,
And change all its greenness to white.
Then home he will go and laugh ho, ho ho
What fun I have had in the night!

Cecily E. Pike, "Jack Frost"

$\mathcal{H}$E'D BEEN! Jack Frost had come during the night, coating the garden with sparkling silver, and painting icy, fern-like patterns on the window pane. As Arthur opened the curtain on that freezing February morning, he smiled to himself before quietly creeping out of the bedroom so as not to disturb Daisy. He remembered his father telling him eerie bedtime stories about the shadowy, elf-like Jack Frost – just as he had to his own children!

Downstairs in the back room, he stoked up the embers of the coal fire that he'd dampened down the night before. How chilly it had been here on winter mornings in the old days, fighting for space among a gaggle of brothers and sisters all crowding round the fire as they dressed. He could picture their faces glowing red from the flames while their backs shivered with cold from the rest of the room. Thick clothes were definitely needed, though, before anyone dared take a trip to the outside privy, which was absolutely perishing on those early winter mornings.

So it was with a quiet sense of pride that Arthur headed towards what, until five years earlier, had been just the back wall of the kitchen, but now, he opened a door to step straight into their brand new bathroom. Jack Frost had peeped through the window of that room too, but it soon warmed up once Arthur had pumped and lit the small paraffin heater there. It had been quite a job to knock down the walls between the old scullery, coal hole and privy, but the room he'd managed to create had just enough space for an enamel bath, WC and sink, into which he now poured hot water straight from the tap.

Catching a glimpse of himself in the mirror above the sink, he grimaced, thinking he always looked terrible first thing in the morning, but perhaps not so bad for a man who had just clocked up his half-century! After a quick shave and a brew of tea, he left a cuppa on Daisy's bedside table before pulling his coat collar up around his ears and heading off to work.

1957

Weather means more when you have a garden. There's nothing like listening to a shower and thinking how it is soaking in around your green beans.

Marcelene Cox

Tommy stepped out of the house into a downpour. Green beans might flourish in this weather, he thought grumpily, but blue suede shoes definitely didn't mix with British rain. The lads were all going to the Backstreet Club that night, where the small dance floor would be packed with rock 'n' rollers, all jiving to the latest hits. Tommy had got his dancing style off to a tee, leading his jive partner with just a flick of the wrist here and an over-the-shoulder lift or a through-the-legs slide there. And if he was to have any chance of grabbing a girl who was half decent, he had to look the part. Soggy shoes were a definite no-no.

He'd been working up to this for almost a year now, and by the time "Heartbreak Hotel" topped the British charts in May 1957, Tommy had already kitted himself out to look as much like his hero, Elvis Presley, as an eighteen-year-old lad in a Medway town could manage. That American baby who could have died along with his twin in Mississippi back in 1935 was certainly making his mark on the world now – especially on Tommy! To the great annoyance of his sister Alice, Tommy spent ages in the bathroom painstakingly slicking his hair back with Brylcream, leaving the obligatory quiff at the front. Once he'd completed the look, with the tight trousers, thick-soled shoes and jacket collar turned up at just the right angle, he reckoned it was hard to tell the difference between him and his idol. Of course, a cigarette smoked with the casual style of James Dean was quite a winner with the girls too, but he reckoned his mum would kill him if she ever found his supply of Willy Woodbines.

"Tommy thinks I don't know he smokes," mused Daisy, as she and Emily heard the front door slam.

"Do you mind?"

"I'd prefer he smoked those new menthols," replied Daisy. "The adverts say they make you breathe more easily."

"In the war," said Emily, "there were adverts telling us we should *all* smoke to calm our nerves."

"And did it?"

"No. The only thing that's ever calmed my nerves is a nice strong cup of tea…"

"… sitting out on the bench in the back yard, chatting to neighbours over the fence…" grinned Daisy.

"… moaning about our men, putting the world to rights!"

Daisy threw her head back and laughed. "That still works for me!"

"Tom spent hours on that bench, smoking his pipe and just staring at his plants as if he thought that would make them grow faster."

"Arthur does much the same now," mused Daisy. "I reckon men become more and more like their dads, especially once they've reached their fifties."

Smiling as she nodded agreement, Emily was sitting in the high-backed chair Tom had loved best because, from it, he could look out through the back room window down the length of his beloved garden at the same time as putting his feet up in front of the fire.

"And a little bit of rain never put either of them off going out to do a bit of digging," she said, "father *or* son."

"Arthur gets quite excited if he sees a black cloud on its way, because it will make the digging easier."

Emily chuckled. "Is it us, or are those men of ours completely mad?"

"Well, we married 'em!" grinned Daisy, getting to her feet. "I could do with a brew now. How about you?"

*More and more I am coming to the conclusion that rain is
a far more important consideration to gardens than sun,
and that one of the lesser advantages that a gardener gains
in life is the thorough enjoyment of a rainy day!*

**Margaret Waterfield, from Flower Grouping in English,
Scotch & Irish Gardens**

৵৻

*Flowers have an expression of countenance as much
as men or animals. Some seem to smile; some have a sad
expression; some are pensive and diffident; others are plain,
honest and upright, like the broad faced sunflower and
the hollyhock.*

*Henry Ward Beecher, "Star Papers:
Or, Experiences of Art and Nature", 1855*

Arthur wasn't sure if he smiled as he gardened, but he *felt* as if
he did, always aware of the deepest sense of contentment as the
physical effort demanded his total concentration. Over the years,
he'd found himself accepting that certain areas of the garden
created a particular mood, and it changed with the seasons. The
yellow and purple irises that filled a cool, out-of-the-way corner

with regal splendour in late spring gave way to summer bedding plants, vibrant and cheerful as they tilted their bright faces towards the sun. And as the kaleidoscope of summer colour faded, the nip of autumn dabbed orange and brown patches on the crisp edges of the trees and hedges. There was never a dull moment in the garden as every tiny seed and elderly shrub came to life, flourished and faded away in a miracle of timing and need.

To every thing there is a season, and a time to every
purpose under the heaven:
A time to be born, and a time to die; a time to plant, and
a time to pluck up that which is planted;
A time to kill, and a time to heal; a time to break down,
and a time to build up;
A time to weep, and a time to laugh; a time to mourn, and
a time to dance;
A time to cast away stones, and a time to gather stones
together; a time to embrace, and a time to refrain from
embracing;
A time to get, and a time to lose; a time to keep, and a
time to cast away;
A time to rend, and a time to sew; a time to keep silence,
and a time to speak;
A time to love, and a time to hate; a time of war, and a
time of peace.

Ecclesiastes 3:1–8

Arthur reached down to pick a fat red strawberry, its sweet juice dripping down his chin as he bit into it. He nodded with satisfaction. It was a good crop this year. It made him think of that other verse, which came a little later in the passage from Ecclesiastes, about there being a season for everything:

And also that every man should eat and drink, and enjoy the good of all his labour, it is the gift of God.

Ecclesiastes 3:13

Amen to that, he thought, as he grabbed a punnet. They'd have strawberries for tea!

1960

It's cherry pink and apple blossom white
When your true lover comes your way
It's cherry pink and apple blossom white
The poets say

The story goes that once a cherry tree
Beside an apple tree did grow
And there a boy once met his bride to be
Long long ago

The boy looked into her eyes, it was a sight to enthral
The breezes joined in their sighs, the blossoms started to fall
And as they gently caressed, the lovers looked up to find
The branches of the two trees were intertwined,

And that is why the poets always write
If there's a new moon bright above
It's cherry pink and apple blossom white
When you're in love

Mack David, "Cherry Pink (And Apple Blossom White)"

The instrumental version of this song, featuring trumpeter Billy Regis, who started each verse with a mood-setting slide up and down his trumpet, had topped the charts for nearly three months – and it summed up the mood in 1960, in the month of May. Fragrant blossom was in the air – and so was romance, as family televisions up and down the country tuned in to watch the wedding of Princess Margaret to Anthony Armstrong-Jones.

Once the royal couple had left the abbey and disappeared into Buckingham Palace for lunch, Alice found a space on the garden bench next to her Auntie Elsie, where they both sat under an arch of pink and white blossom.

"Aunt Elsie," Alice started, "do you think I'm an old spinster? I turned twenty-six last month."

Elsie snorted with laughter. "No! Whatever makes you ask that?"

"Jimmy's asked me to marry him."

"Do you love him?"

"Yes."

"Enough to want to wake up beside him every morning for the rest of your life?"

Alice opened her mouth to reply, then thought better of it.

"You worked hard for that home economics diploma of yours," continued Elsie. "A qualification like that could take you a long way. What did you have in mind when you started it?"

Elsie watched her niece's face carefully as she replied.

"I rather liked the idea of becoming a teacher, perhaps in one of the new comprehensives."

"So what are you doing about that?"

"Nothing now. Jimmy doesn't think his wife should work. He says a woman's place is in the home looking after the children."

"And what do you think?"

Alice took a while to consider her answer. "I think I'd like to teach home economics in one of those comprehensives."

"And would Jimmy encourage that, knowing how much it means to you?"

"I don't know. I've never had the courage to ask him."

"Well, perhaps you should, before he puts a ring on your finger."

Alice nodded thoughtfully as the two women fell silent, watching petals of blossom tumble down on the breeze.

"Can I ask you something?" began Alice at last. "It's a question you may not want to answer."

"Fire away," replied Elsie, plainly intrigued.

"You never had children, and yet you've always been everyone's favourite auntie. Didn't you want any of your own?"

"I did. It just never happened. I used to mind a lot about it, but time's a good healer."

"What about Uncle Sam? Men always want a son to carry on the family name, don't they?"

"Sam loves me. I couldn't have children, but he still loved me. Yes, I think it was a great sadness for him – for both of us – but I've learned that life has a way of compensating for disappointments."

"Your work?"

"Yes. When Sam made me a partner in our solicitors' practice, even though I wasn't qualified in law as he was, he did me the honour of recognizing that my contribution to the success of the business was as important as his. And then, when I was elected a town councillor, well, I felt I'd been given the chance to speak up for this town I love, for the people I've grown up with, the schools that taught me, the workers who deserve to earn a decent wage to live on."

"What you do matters," said Alice. "I want to do something that matters too, not just for me, but for other people as well."

"Teaching matters."

"It does," Alice agreed.

"And you're not an old spinster. You are a young woman with a lifetime of opportunity ahead of you. Marriage may be part of that, but only marry someone if, when you're together, you complete each other – someone you can't live without!"

"Like Uncle Sam?"

Elsie smiled. "Yes, like my Sam."

1961

Gather ye rosebuds while ye may,
Old Time is still a-flying;
And this same flower that smiles today
Tomorrow will be dying.

Robert Herrick, "To the Virgins, to Make Much of Time"

Emily insisted she didn't want a fuss, but the family were determined to mark her ninetieth birthday with a proper celebration. They wanted to hire a local hall, but Emily wouldn't hear of it, and finally it was agreed that a buffet tea would be organized at home. That did mean, though, that Emily assumed *she* would be preparing the spread for the party, as she had for so many years, which Arthur found very alarming. In the end, Daisy suggested a compromise, with Emily making the fruit cake, trifle and bread pudding, which were her speciality, leaving all the other family members to bring along a varied mix of their own creations.

Alice, who masterminded it all, was on hand to take a picture of the buffet before they tucked in. There were pineapple, cheese and silverskin onion hedgehogs, prawn cocktail sandwiches, cheese straws, Black Forest gateau, Battenberg cake, egg and bacon flan, and circles of beautifully arranged lettuce, cucumber, spring onions and tomatoes (all from Arthur's garden, of course) topped by bright yellow rings of hard-boiled egg.

"She should take this up professionally, don't you think?" whispered Elsie to the tall man who was watching Alice skilfully serving up portions of cold meat and potato salad.

Michael, who was the deputy headmaster of the local comprehensive school, smiled in agreement. "She's very talented. Creating a magnificent buffet is second nature to her."

"You eat well then!"

He laughed. "I've never been so spoiled, but I'm quite happy to sort out the evening meal for us both if I get home before her."

"You're what they call *a new man* then, are you?" asked Elsie.

"Alice and I think of ourselves as equal partners. Does that make me a new man?"

"Probably. Especially as you two modern young things are living in sin! What does Arthur think about that?"

"I've never dared ask him," grinned Michael.

"Well, let me dare ask you: are you two planning to have children?"

"Probably, but only if Alice is okay with that."

"And what happens if you have a slip-up? Would you stand by her?"

"There won't be a slip-up. She's on the pill."

Elsie laughed. "It really is a whole new world, isn't it? You make me feel old!"

"Who's old?" asked Emily, who was sitting in her usual chair by the back room window.

"Not you, Mum!" replied Elsie. "You never seem to change."

"Where did the years go, Elsie? It seems no time ago that I was sitting in this chair nursing you, and all the others."

"You made a happy home for us here, Mum."

"I miss him every day, you know."

"Dad?"

Emily nodded. "Tom was a good man. I look forward to being with him again."

Elsie frowned. "Don't wish your life away, Mum."

"Why not? Are we talking about a wish for *me*, or for *you*?"

Elsie knelt down until she was level with Emily, and simply took her mother in her arms.

"For all of us. You're very loved. Never forget that."

1964

Bo and Dora's son David was a regular visitor to see his gran Emily, often brought over in the car by one of his older twin sisters, Christine, who was now the mum of a lively four-year-old daughter, Judith, and baby John who was coming up to his first birthday.

When they called in one Friday evening, Emily and Arthur were settled back in their armchairs watching their favourite BBC presenter Percy Thrower on *Gardening Club*. Suddenly, David walked into the room, music blaring from his transistor radio even though it was glued to his ear.

"I can't hear the television!" grumbled Arthur.

"But *this* is what you should be listening to, Uncle Arthur!" retorted David, turning the volume up even louder. "This group are brilliant! They're called The Beatles."

"How nice," was Arthur's acid reply. "Can you turn that radio off now so that your gran and I can hear the television?"

"But just listen! Their songs are so good, even *you* might like them. This one's great – '... *with love from me to you*'".

"What I will be giving you, with love from me to you, is a thick ear if you don't turn that music off this instant, you cheeky blighter!"

Just at that moment, Daisy walked into the room, surprised to hear her husband raising his voice. She was followed by their son Tommy, who was just popping in to say goodbye before heading out on the motorbike that was his pride and joy. He grimaced when he heard the music.

"For pity's sake, David, that's such a row! Only *girls* like that rubbishy stuff! When are you going to grow up and realize that proper men like rock 'n' roll?"

"He's a Rocker, Gran," explained David patiently. "Poor old souls, they're stuck back in the fifties. Those of us who are *really* with it appreciate a more modern style – like The Beatles..."

"David, David," moaned Tommy, "what am I going to do with you? Call yourself a *Mod*, do you? All perfume and backcombed hair?"

David brushed down his high-collared jacket with pride. "A dedicated follower of fashion, that's me. Look, Uncle Arthur, I've even got flowers on my shirt. Patterns like this are all the rage at the moment."

"The rage will be all mine, dear David," replied Arthur coolly, "if you don't take your flowery shirt away from the television screen so that I can see Percy Thrower talking sense about *real* flowers."

"Yes, just push off, Dave," snapped Tommy rudely. "Pansies aren't welcome here."

"Oh, I wouldn't say that," said Arthur. "I'm rather partial to a tub of winter pansies. Now clear off, both of you, and let me watch my programme in peace!"

It was very clear where all the young men had gone just a few weeks later over the Whitsun Bank Holiday when the television evening news programme showed shocking footage of hundreds of Mods and Rockers descending on the nearby holiday town of Margate for a day out at the seaside. Rockers roared down the road to the coast in black swarms of heavy-metal motorbikes, while the Mods arrived on their Vespa and Lambretta scooters, many with long-haired, dolly-bird girlfriends riding pillion. In the running battle that erupted, the Rockers dug out bike chains and knuckle-dusters from their leather jackets, while Mods produced razor blades that had been sewn into their suit lapels.

Knowing that Tommy had been heading for Margate with his own biker friends, Arthur and Daisy waited up until three in the morning before they heard his key in the door. He was limping and had a nasty gash on his cheekbone from being thumped by a sharp strip of wood from a broken deckchair.

"I'm ashamed of you, Tommy," said Arthur. "We didn't bring you up to behave like that towards anyone, whatever you think of their choices or style."

"Well, if you don't like the company I keep and you're not interested in the things that matter to me," snapped Tommy, "I'd better leave."

And turning on his heel, he slammed the front door so hard that the whole house shook as he stormed out.

1965

Three days before her ninety-fourth birthday, Emily thought it looked warm enough outside for her to take a slow walk down the garden path to sit in the sunshine. She might have called for Daisy to lend her an arm, but she knew her daughter-in-law was busy upstairs, and every step Emily took down the path to the bench was dear and familiar to her.

She felt the silky leaves of the bay tree plant that had always been outside the back door to bring good fortune to the family home. She touched the bird table Tom had made years ago, and ran her fingers across the pink honeysuckle and fragrant jasmine that covered the side fence. She glanced over to the rockery, peppered with tufts of London Pride and rock daisies with splashes of pink phlox and soft green hostas between its grey boulders. She peered into the greenhouse where Arthur's prize chrysanthemums were already in bud, ready to bloom just in time for the flower show. Then she pottered on towards the back fence, picturing how busy the coal depot had been when she first came to this house. Homes had central heating now, and coal arrived in thick pre-packed plastic bags, resulting in the depot being eerily silent.

She took her time getting back to the bench, and sank gratefully into her favourite spot in the garden. A smile crept across her face thinking of Tom in his battered old hat and garden boots jamming the spade into the hard ground as he began to tame the wasteland this garden used to be.

A movement caught her eye. Wobin had come to perch alongside her on the arm of the bench, his head tilted, a knowing look of kindness in his unblinking stare.

"It's been good, Wobin, hasn't it?" she whispered.

A beam of sunlight suddenly burst through a shift in the clouds, and she closed her eyes against the dazzling light, breathing in the sweet scent of Ernest's white rose bush.

Tom planted that, she thought, feeling warm and drowsy as her head dropped in sleep.

She never woke up again.

1966

It's all I have to bring today –
This, and my heart beside –
This, and my heart, and all the fields –
And all the meadows wide –
Be sure you count – should I forget
Some one the sum could tell –
This, and my heart, and all the Bees
Which in the Clover dwell.

Emily Dickinson,
"It's all I have to bring today"

DAISY REACHED INTO the sleeve of her new mint-coloured silk suit to find the embroidered handkerchief she had hidden there. Beside her in the front pew of the church, Elsie stretched across to clasp Daisy's hand as the two of them watched Alice walk down the aisle on Arthur's arm. Elsie thought she had never seen her niece look more serene and beautiful. Who cared that it had taken all of her thirty-two years before she'd felt able to take this step? In the end, Michael was the one – the one she had chosen to live with for the past two years; the one she knew she couldn't live without.

Pacing his steps to the exact tempo of Wagner's "Wedding March", Arthur found his eyes drawn to the face of his old friend, the statue of Christ that stood above the altar. Their relationship over the years had had its ups and downs, but the older he became, the more he valued Christ's presence in his life. The simple truths of the Bible that his mother had taught him as a child – the commands that he should love his neighbour and always try to see another's point of view before he condemned or judged, and most of all the responsibility he'd instinctively felt to recognize and nurture even the smallest miracles of God's creation – those principles had shaped his life. And it had been a long life now. He'd turned sixty this year, a milestone he wasn't completely sure he welcomed.

The happy couple had chosen a nearby country hotel for their reception, and family and friends gathered round in the sunshine, sipping sherry as they waited to be called for photographs.

Daisy smiled in welcome when Tommy came across holding his new-born son Matthew in his arms, his wife Belinda beside him. As Daisy joined them to coo and gush over her first grandchild, Arthur found himself smiling at the memory of Tommy two years earlier, the angry young man who'd got into a fight and stormed out of his family home. In some ways, that outburst had been the making of him. He had moved into a flat with his friend Bob, who worked as a telephone engineer for the Post Office. Two months later, when Tommy had been taken on as one of Bob's team of engineers, he'd not only found a career he really enjoyed, but the girl he loved too: Bob's sister Belinda. From the moment they'd met her, Arthur and Daisy were drawn to the girl's warm smile, her down-to-earth ways and the fact that she plainly adored their son. Their registry office wedding was the low-key affair they both wanted before they moved into a rented ground-floor maisonette not far from the family home.

The delicious aroma of roast dinner in the oven welcomed Daisy and Arthur as they arrived at the maisonette one Sunday for lunch. Belinda greeted them both with a hug just as Tommy called to his dad from their pocket-sized back garden.

"What should I do with these, Dad? I thought tomato seeds were supposed to be easy to grow, but my plants are so spindly!"

Daisy almost laughed out loud to hear their conversation. In her mind's eye, she pictured the little boy Tommy had been, bored and fidgeting whenever Arthur tried to interest his son in gardening. And now look at the two of them, in deep discussion about fruit and veg!

"Well, you see, son, these modern tomato seeds are hybrids, not a patch on the old varieties that are tougher and have so much more flavour. I could bring a few seeds over for you when I next come – and maybe you'd like to try your hand at some beans and peas too…"

Arthur didn't know if the smile in his heart actually reached his face, but it was with a glow of pride and contentment that he knelt down beside his son to pass on a little gardening advice, just as his own dad had to him.

I dug
I levelled
I weeded
I seeded
I planted
I waited
I weeded
I pleaded
I mulched
I gulched
I watered
I waited
I fumbled
I grumbled
I poked
I hoped
so GROW... dammit.

**Marian French,
"Gardener's Complaint"**

On the 30th July 1966, just two weeks after Alice and Michael's wedding, the old family house was packed. Ever since Arthur had ordered their first television set for the Queen's Coronation back in 1953, it had been the tradition that if there was a big football match, the men of the family gathered at the house to watch it together, along with copious supplies of beer, roasted peanuts in their shells, and bags of plain potato crisps with little blue packets of salt inside to add flavour. The atmosphere was electric, full of excited anticipation, as they joined the other thirty-two million people who watched England play West Germany in the World Cup Final that day. The England squad, which included great players like brothers Jack and Bobby Charlton, Bobby Moore, Alan Ball and Nobby Stiles, knew they were the underdogs, but the home crowd roared support for their team as they marched onto the pitch at their beloved old Wembley Stadium. The match was an emotional roller-coaster, full of twists and turns, but when Geoff Hurst clinched a home win with his unbelievable hat-trick of goals, the first ever scored in a World Cup Final, the cheer that erupted at Wembley shook the country from one end to the other.

It seemed that life couldn't get any better during that feel-good year. Just weeks before, the country had cheered at the other unexpected triumph, when popular home-grown boxer Henry

Cooper actually *floored* World Heavyweight Champion Cassius Clay during a title match watched by a crowd of 40,000 at Arsenal's stadium in Highbury. Henry didn't win, but after that performance he was the nation's hero anyway!

And Britain was leading the way in style, especially with The Beatles dominating the world music scene with every album they released. And the Beach Boys might have been singing about the charms of their "California Girls" just a few months earlier, but when it came to micro mini-skirts and cheeky style, there were none to beat the British girls epitomized by stick-thin model Twiggy, with her short angular haircut and enormous black-ringed eyes. Shops were full of tight trousers flared at the knee, peasant blouses and suede knee-high boots. It was a time for flowers in your hair and joy in your heart. Finally, after all the dark years everyone had been through, things were beginning to brighten up…

Be like the flower, turn your face to the sun.

Kahlil Gibran

1969

"Good morning, Arthur."

He looked up from tucking tendrils of his bean plants around their bamboo cane supports to see Peggy's head peeping over the side fence. She had only been their next-door neighbour for a year or so, since her husband Colin retired from working on merchant ships. Having lived all over the world because of his job, he decided to spend his long-awaited retirement in the town that had been a childhood home for both him and Peggy – except that, just a matter of weeks after the couple had moved in, a massive and totally unexpected heart attack claimed his life. Peggy had been devastated by the loss, and she wondered how she could ever have coped with the shock and grief without the loving support of her son and family, who lived in a small village about twenty miles away. They had immediately suggested that she come to live with them, but Peggy resisted.

"Colin and I came home when we chose this house," she explained to Daisy over the garden fence. "We didn't want to live in the country. We wanted to live here, in a street just like this, around the corner from where our homes used to be before the war. I know the family mean well, but I'm not ready to give up that dream yet. Colin wouldn't want me to."

So Arthur and Daisy had quietly kept a watchful eye on their elderly neighbour, inviting her over for tea, helping her with shopping, and handing bunches of flowers and freshly picked vegetables over the fence. Her own garden was basic and sparse, with a ragged length of grass filling most of it, and cracks in the concrete that stretched from outside the kitchen door right down the overgrown path. Every now and then, Arthur would spend an afternoon pruning the ivy that was laying claim to the back wall of her house at an alarming rate, and tackling the weeds that were growing much stronger and faster than any of the plants that were *supposed* to be in her garden.

"I just want to say," said Peggy that morning, "how much I appreciate your garden from this side of the fence – and even better when I look down on it from my bedroom window. I know I have a long way to go before my little patch is even half decent, but I get so much pleasure just from seeing how *your* garden grows!"

Arthur was taken aback by her kind words.

"Your garden is a gift to me, Arthur, and it brings me joy every day. It is another example of your friendship, which I appreciate so much."

And with that, her head disappeared, leaving Arthur staring after her wordlessly, a knot of emotion like a lump in his throat.

The roses red upon my neighbour's vine
Are owned by him, but they are also mine.
His was the cost, and his the labour, too,
But mine as well as his the joy, their loveliness to view.
They bloom for me and are for me as fair
As for the man who gives them all his care.
Thus I am rich, because a good man grew
A rose-clad vine for all his neighbour's view.

I know from this that others plant for me,
And what they own, my joy may also be.
So why be selfish, when so much that's fine
Is grown for you, upon your neighbour's vine.

Abraham L. Gruber, "My Neighbour's Roses"

1969

On the 16th July 1969, the world held its breath as news broke of Apollo II's take-off with three American astronauts on board. Four days later, television screens were filled with images of Neil Armstrong stepping down from the spacecraft to become the first man to walk on the moon.

"That's one small step for a man, one giant leap for mankind," he said, as his foot touched the moon's surface with the whole world watching.

Later that evening, Arthur wandered down to the middle of his garden, where he stopped to look up at the moon, scanning it to see if it looked different after the momentous events of the day. He chuckled to himself. How ridiculous to think he would be able to see anything different at all – and yet, from that day, everything *would* be very different. His grandchildren would live in a world where space travel was a part of everyday life, offering endless possibilities, hopefully for the good of all mankind. Would the world be wise enough to investigate those possibilities with care – or would the promise of life beyond our planet be yet another reason for country to rival country to possess and dominate what lay above and around us all?

Arthur sank onto the bench, looking up at the sparkling sky, as he had done all his life. When he was a boy, he imagined that what he was glimpsing up there was heaven itself, and even now he liked to think of the brightest stars as those he'd loved and lost – his father, brother Ernest and, all too recently, his darling mum. Science had its value, he thought, but instinct mattered too – and instinctively he knew that, here in the garden he cherished and nurtured, he was watched over and cared for by eternal and unconditional love.

A black cat among roses,
Phlox, lilac-misted under a first-quarter moon,
The sweet smells of heliotrope and night-scented stock.
The garden is very still,
It is dazed with moonlight,
Contented with perfume,
Dreaming the opium dreams of its folded poppies.
Firefly lights open and vanish
High as the tip buds of the golden glow
Low as the sweet alyssum flowers at my feet.
Moon-shimmer on leaves and trellises,
Moon-spikes shafting through the snow ball bush.
Only the little faces of the ladies' delight are alert and
staring,

Only the cat, padding between the roses,
Shakes a branch and breaks the chequered pattern
As water is broken by the falling of a leaf.
Then you come,
And you are quiet like the garden,
And white like the alyssum flowers,
And beautiful as the silent sparks of the fireflies.
Ah, Beloved, do you see those orange lilies?
They knew my mother,
But who belonging to me will they know
When I am gone.

Amy Lowell, "The Garden by Moonlight"

1971

On his sixty-fifth birthday on the 3rd April, men from almost every department in the dockyard crowded into the canteen for Arthur's retirement ceremony. There was a birthday cake, cups of tea and coffee, sandwiches and biscuits, reminiscences, laughter and very kind words from the Chief Executive before he presented Arthur with a gold watch inscribed *Arthur Freeman, Chatham Dockyard 1923–1971.* And then, with a card signed by more than a hundred workmates whose lives he'd shared for nearly half a century, he cleared out his locker, gave back the key and headed home.

Daisy met him at their front gate, holding her arms open so he could simply walk into them.

"Come on," she whispered in his ear, "we've got liver and bacon for tea – your favourite."

1972

Arthur could hear Lyn Anderson singing the hit "I Never Promised You a Rose Garden" on Daisy's radio in the kitchen as he led Matthew and Claire out to the potting shed. Tommy's children were growing fast. Matthew had been at school for a year now, and his little sister Claire was four, so would be joining the reception class after Christmas.

"There you are," said Arthur, helping Claire up onto a stool so that she could reach the potting table properly.

"I've got the jam jars ready, and here are the sheets of blotting paper you need to fold into a circle to put inside each jar."

Claire chewed her bottom lip in concentration, finally producing a much neater finish than big brother Matthew, who never stopped talking and was all fingers and thumbs as he squashed the blotting paper awkwardly into the jar.

"And here," announced Arthur, producing a broad bean from a small coloured envelope with a flourish, "is what we're going to be growing in the jars. See the picture on the front of the packet? Do you remember me showing you beans like these in their pods last year when you helped me pick them for Sunday lunch?"

Claire looked puzzled, but Matthew's head nodded furiously just to make sure Grandad knew *he* remembered, even if his sister didn't.

"Right! Here are three beans for each of you. Push them halfway down the jar, between the paper and the glass."

"They're falling down!" whined Matthew. "Mine keep falling to the bottom of the jar!"

Arthur leaned over his grandson's shoulders, guiding Matthew's fingers as he retrieved the beans, then wedged them against the glass with the blotting paper.

"Now we just need to soak the paper to give the beans a good drink – and this is something you'll have to do every day when the jars are on your windowsill at home. Those beans need lots of water to make them grow fast!"

"I want to do some more!" squealed Matthew, hopping from foot to foot with excitement. "What can I plant? These?"

He picked up a small brown wages envelope that Arthur grabbed with alarm before last year's precious tomato seeds were spilled all over the floor.

"Maybe not those, but how about these?" he suggested, holding up a bright yellow packet. "Do you know what these flowers are?"

Both children looked blankly at the picture on the packet cover.

"They're sunflowers," explained Arthur. "They have big golden faces that can be as wide as a dinner plate!"

"Wow!" gasped Matthew.

"And they will grow taller than you, Claire."

"Not me though!" interrupted Matthew. "I'm the tallest boy in my class."

"And these will be the tallest flowers in the garden in a couple of months' time – taller than you, and probably taller than me too!"

"Wow!" cried Matthew again, trying rather unsuccessfully to imagine a plant taller than Grandad.

"We need to put them in separate little pots like the ones I've got here, and when the plants are big and strong enough, we can turn them out and dig them into the garden."

"Wow!" said Matthew a third time. "I'm going to tell Daddy!"

"Let's plant the seeds first," laughed Arthur. "Then you two can call Daddy to show him how clever you've been!"

In the heart of the seed
Buried deep so deep
A dear little plant
Lay fast asleep.

"Wake," said the sunshine,
"And creep to the light."
"Wake," said the voice
Of the raindrops bright.

The little plant heard
And it rose to see
What a wonderful sight,
The outside world might be.

Kate Louise Brown, "The Plant Baby and Its Friends"

1972

As Daisy raised her glass to Bo and Dora in celebration of their Silver Wedding anniversary, she found it hard to believe that it was more than twenty-five years since Bo, the youngest sibling in Arthur's generation of the family, had returned traumatized and broken after his time as a Japanese prisoner-of-war. It was nothing less than a miracle to see him now, toned and well weathered from running his own building company for the last two decades. If only Emily and Tom could see him now! In fact, how much they would have loved to see all their family that day, enjoying each other's company along with their children and grandchildren.

She'd noticed a definite family look, both in men and women, among the Freeman clan as they grew older, and Arthur was a perfect example of that. Now aged sixty-six, his hair was still thick and strong, although it had been snowy white for some time, a striking contrast to those pale blue eyes of his. And there could be no mistaking any of his brothers and sisters because, as Arthur laughingly said, they all looked like peas in a pod!

The anniversary party was being held in a large upper room in one of the local pubs, and nearly all the guests lived locally, with the notable exception of Dick, the oldest boy since the death of Ernest in the Great War. He'd travelled down from London with his wife Audrey, who refused several family offers of a bed for the night in favour of staying in the only four-star hotel within reasonable distance.

"She's a bit above herself, don't you think?" said Daisy.

"A stuck-up little minx," agreed Elsie, a gin and tonic in her hand. "Do you know she'll *only* call him Richard, when he's been Dick to all of us for as long as we've known him? She obviously thinks Richard makes him sound a bit grander."

"He's still our own boy, though, isn't he," said Ada, who at seventy-two was the eldest of all the siblings. "She may have airs and graces, but he seems as down-to-earth as ever."

"Who else is there to gossip about?" mused Elsie, scanning the room. "I like what Dora's chosen to wear for her anniversary party. Usually she dresses in colours that allow her to fade into the background, but she's the belle of the ball tonight in that yellow dress and jacket."

"She does look lovely," agreed Daisy.

"And I see that Bo's invited his pals from the Wheatsheaf!"

"Well, he's in the pub darts team there," explained Daisy. "Dora told me they're in the county league at the moment, and are hoping to win the cup!"

But Elsie's beady eyes had already moved on from the Wheatsheaf crowd towards the table that she and her husband Sam had joined. Sam was in deep conversation there with a middle-aged couple sitting alongside him.

"That's Councillor Frank Baker," explained Elsie. "Do you know him?"

"Only by reputation. Is he on the same side of the council as you?"

"No, but politics apart, he's a good man who really cares for the people of the town."

"And the woman across from him? I don't recognize her."

"That's Barbara Warwick – you know she runs her own accountancy practice in the town? Bo's building business is one of the many on her books."

"She looks really elegant."

"Oh, you'll never see Barbara with even one hair out of place.

She's a smart one, that lady, and not just in the way she dresses. I would say she has a very clear view of her career path."

"Is she married?" asked Daisy.

"I don't think a husband is likely to feature on that career path of hers – unless he's loaded!"

Daisy laughed. "That's probably where I went wrong. My mum told me to marry man with a few beans to his name. I took her literally and married Arthur!"

Elsie nearly choked on her drink as the two women giggled together.

"I think that makes you a very smart woman indeed!"

A single flow'r he sent me, since we met.
All tenderly his messenger he chose;
Deep-hearted, pure, with scented dew still wet –
One perfect rose.

I knew the language of the floweret;
"My fragile leaves," it said, "his heart enclose."
Love long has taken for his amulet
One perfect rose.

Why is it no one ever sent me yet
One perfect limousine, do you suppose?
Ah no, it's always just my luck to get
One perfect rose.

Dorothy Parker, "One Perfect Rose"

1976

I remember, I remember,
The house where I was born,
The little window where the sun
Came peeping in at morn;
He never came a wink too soon,
Nor brought too long a day;
But now, I often wish the night
Had borne my breath away!

I remember, I remember,
The roses, red and white,

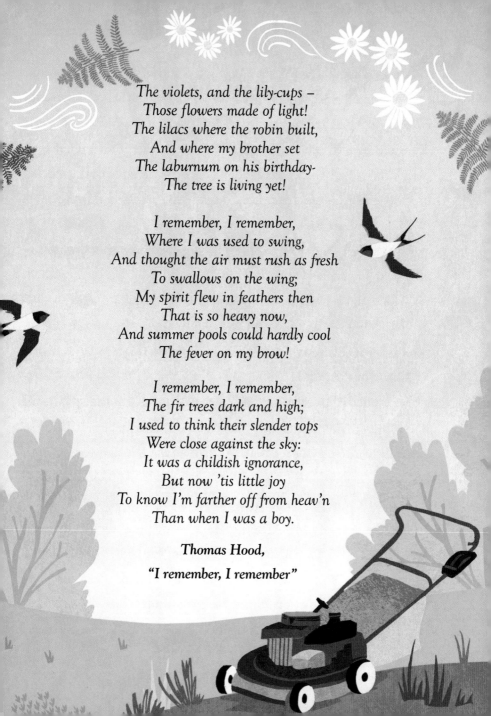

The violets, and the lily-cups –
Those flowers made of light!
The lilacs where the robin built,
And where my brother set
The laburnum on his birthday-
The tree is living yet!

I remember, I remember,
Where I was used to swing,
And thought the air must rush as fresh
To swallows on the wing;
My spirit flew in feathers then
That is so heavy now,
And summer pools could hardly cool
The fever on my brow!

I remember, I remember,
The fir trees dark and high;
I used to think their slender tops
Were close against the sky:
It was a childish ignorance,
But now 'tis little joy
To know I'm farther off from heav'n
Than when I was a boy.

Thomas Hood,

"I remember, I remember"

THE SUMMER OF 1976 was one of the hottest anyone could remember, and when Daisy brought Arthur a glass of cold elderflower cordial made from the white flower heads she'd collected from the back lane a few weeks earlier, they pulled up a couple of wrought-iron metal chairs to the little table in the yard to enjoy their drink together.

"The garden's looking nice," said Daisy.

"It's dry," Arthur sighed. "I can hardly keep up with the watering when the days are so long and hot."

"Does that new hose system of yours work well?"

"It's doing a grand job on the vegetables, but I prefer to do the flowers with a watering can."

"Like your dad did…"

He smiled. "Yes, like dad did, because he swore that plants all need different amounts of water to keep them happy. If I dowse them all with the hose, I could drown some of the more delicate ones."

"I'm sure your dad would be pleased with what you've done."

"Do you reckon so? I think about him a lot when I'm out here. He was only a simple working man, but he had good instincts when it came to gardening."

"Green fingers?"

"He was green all through, I reckon!"

"Like his son! And Tommy too, it seems? He's doing well with that garden of theirs."

There was a touch of pride in Arthur's voice as he answered. "He is. The gardening bug's taken a bit of time to reach him, but I think he's well and truly bitten now!"

"A chip off the old block, eh?" grinned Daisy.

Arthur chuckled. "Well, gardening is a hard labour of love, so it's not for everyone."

"That's true," she agreed. "But I know a few women round here who would love to have more time to potter in the garden, but they have enough on their hands bringing up the family, running the house and sometimes holding down their own job as well."

"It would seem odd to me," said Arthur thoughtfully, "that it would be the woman rather than the man of the house who'd want to do all that digging and muck-raking. That's hardly women's work!"

"*Everything* is women's work, my darling!" smiled Daisy. "Don't you remember that song by Helen Reddy a few years back – 'I am woman, I am invincible…'?"

"I am man," grinned Arthur. "I am the boss. My wife told me so!"

1977

And some can pot begonias and some can bud a rose,
And some are hardly fit to trust with anything
that grows...

Rudyard Kipling, "The Glory of the Garden"

Arthur's next-door neighbour Wilf retired not long after Arthur, but he remained the same happy-go-lucky, delightfully chaotic character he'd been as a lad. Years ago, Emily had called him a "wide boy", always up to some mischief or money-making venture (often one and the same thing when it came to Wilf!) and she'd sometimes worried about whether Wilf's bad habits might rub off on her practical, hard-working son. Nothing had ever dented their friendship, though, and Arthur enjoyed seeing a bit more of Wilf now they were both supposed to be "gentlemen of leisure".

"I've been thinking," said Wilf one morning as he leaned over the fence.

Arthur laughed. "Steady, Tiger!"

"My garden's a mess!"

"That's an understatement if ever I heard one!"

"Would you help me with it?"

"Why? You've never worried about it before."

"Yes, but I'm spending more time at home now and it would be nice to look out on something other than long grass and weeds."

"That's true," nodded Arthur.

"So, how do I get rid of the weeds then?"

"Are you really serious?"

"Of course!"

"And you won't just leave me to do all the work while you watch from the back room with your feet up in front of the telly?"

"Arthur, how could you think such a thing?"

Arthur eyed his friend suspiciously. "Okay," he said at last, "I'll dig out a few tools from the shed, and we'll get started."

A week later, Wilf had gone off gardening altogether, deciding that there was no point in trying to hold back nature when nature would always win. Besides, he reasoned, if dandelions had turned out to be *difficult* to grow, gardeners would probably welcome them on their lawns! With a parting shot over his shoulder that anyone who wasted time on gardening probably needed to lie down in a darkened room with a flannel on their heads, Wilf slammed the kitchen door and took up his usual comfortable spot in front of the television.

It really is quite silly,
If I want to grow a lily,
The time and fuss and effort that
It takes to make a show.
But a buttercup or daisy
Is not at all that lazy;
I can leave it to get on with it
And know that it will grow.

If a rose bush I neglected
It would probably get infected
With a leaf mould or a greenfly
Which would lead to its demise.
But a dandelion don't need it,
I don't have to mulch or feed it,
And I never need to prune it
To manipulate its size.

With a weed there is no weeding,
It's self-sowing and self-seeding,
Quite different from the annuals
I must re-sow every spring.
And I wouldn't need my barrow

With a garden full of yarrow;
I could lie there in my deck chair
And not worry 'bout a thing.

That humble little clover
Could be left to grow all over,
Bringing great delight, I'm certain,
To the butterflies and bees.
It would multiply and flourish,
So I wouldn't need to nourish,
With my poor old back complaining
While I'm down there on my knees.

To waste it is a pity
When oxalis is so pretty
And it never is affected
When the weather brings us storms.
There's no call for manure,
For the spray that's meant to cure
Only helps in distribution
Of its robust little corms.

Should I desire a climber
Then convolvulus, that old-timer,
Would decorate my fences
And enhance my garden wall.
And if I had to shear it
I could hack it, slash it, tear it,
And it wouldn't even shudder,
No, it wouldn't care at all.

Instead of costly, fussy flowers
Which I tend for hours and hours,
My "wild flower" garden would respond
Without much work to do.
If I create some market needs,
Consumer uses for my weeds,
I could sell them off in quantity
And make some money too.

Eunice Perkins, "Why Don't We Grow Weeds"

1978

Country gentlemen may find, in using my machine themselves, an amusing, useful and healthy exercise.

Edwin Beard Budding,
inventor of the lawnmower, from his patent application

Daisy always wondered if, when Tommy and Belinda made the final decision about the house they wanted to buy, the large back garden with its view over the downs clinched the deal for Tommy. Being a very practical person, Belinda got straight to work stripping off the old anaglypta wallpaper, scraping layers of paint off the skirting boards so that they could be sanded back to the original grain and colour of the wood, and running up brightly coloured curtains on Daisy's old sewing machine. Meanwhile, Tommy got cracking with the garden. Their son Matthew, at fourteen, was mostly interested in practising his John Travolta moves since the film *Saturday Night Fever* had hit the cinemas a few weeks earlier, and twelve-year-old Claire was quite a shy girl who mostly had her nose happily buried in a book. That meant the garden was totally Tommy's domain – a thought he relished.

"That's a lot of grass," Arthur commented when he first saw the length of the lawn that stretched in front of them. "Do you want to borrow my lawnmower?"

Tommy looked slightly awkward as he answered. "That's a kind thought, Dad, but I'm not sure your machine would be able to cope with all this."

Arthur chuckled. "You mean it's as archaic as its owner?"

"Of course not," spluttered Tommy. "I just meant…"

"… thank you, but no thanks! It's okay, Tom, I completely understand."

"Well, in that case," replied Tommy, his face suddenly lighting up like a child's at Christmas time, "come and see this!"

Tommy hurried over to the door that led into the garage from the back garden. As his son disappeared inside, Arthur tried to identify the intriguing sounds that preceded Tommy's reappearance. Then he emerged pushing a sparkling, olive-green, state-of-the-art lawnmower.

"My goodness, that's a beauty!" breathed Arthur, bending down to study the machine with admiration. "Have you tried it yet?"

"It only arrived yesterday, so today's the day! It looks easy enough. Do you want a go?"

Arthur stepped back as he stood up. "I wouldn't dream of robbing you of your maiden voyage. Your lawn awaits! I'll sit up by the kitchen there and have a cup of tea as I cheer you on!"

It took a bit of huffing and puffing for Tom to get his technique just right, but two hours later, the lawn was looking immaculate, with smart straight lines right down to the fence at the back.

"Hmm," said Arthur approvingly. "I might have to borrow that. But of course, being an old codger who could so easily chop my toes off with such a new-fangled contraption, I'll have to ask you to bring it round once a week in the summer to mow my lawn for me!"

My neighbour asked if he could use my lawnmower and I told him of course he could, so long as he didn't take it out of my garden.

Eric Morecambe, from the comedy duo Morecambe and Wise

1979

"She's driving me completely mad!" wailed Wilf, shutting the door behind him as he joined Arthur in the greenhouse. "I hardly know the woman! Why should it be me that has to look after her?"

Arthur eyed his friend with sympathy. "She's your cousin, and you're her only living relative."

"Yes, but you could hardly say we're close. I can't look after myself, let alone someone else! Whatever made the hospital think it would be a good idea to send Freda over here after her operation?"

Wondering exactly the same thing, Arthur tried to be encouraging. "It's only for a few weeks, isn't it, until she's mobile enough to go back to her own home?"

"A few weeks of that woman in the house will be the end of me! The district nurse said she has to have a bell at arm's reach so that she can ring whenever she needs me."

"And how's that going?"

"I'm not her butler! And I'm certainly not going to answer a bell."

"So what *are* you doing for her?"

"I'm supposed to help her up in the morning, and then get her downstairs to sit in the back room. She needs breakfast, lunch and tea – and you know I don't do meal times! I just graze all day long. But oh no, that's not good enough for Madam Freda! And then I've got to do her shopping, post her letters, get her washing done… She's even sending me off to buy her fruit & nut bars and packets of wine gums from the shop across the road. And that's all before I have to manhandle her back upstairs again so that she can go to bed."

"So how are you managing?"

A sly smile crept across Wilf's face. "Well, once she's asleep at night, I turn the clock in her room back by two hours, so when she wakes up at eight o'clock, she thinks it's only six and goes back to sleep. And then around teatime, I turn the downstairs clock forward by two hours so that, at six in the evening, I can get her back upstairs because she thinks it's bedtime!"

"Wilf, you don't!"

"Of course not!" he grinned, touching the side of his nose with his finger and winking as he opened the door to leave the greenhouse.

1982

"Is Mum okay?"

Alice asked the question almost under her breath as she and Arthur watched the painful process of Daisy pulling herself out of the chair by the back room window. That was where Tom had loved to sit, followed by Emily after that, but in recent years Daisy had made the chair her own, with its fat, soft cushions and colourful crocheted covers. Arthur remembered her working on those covers, her fingers flying as she wove the needle in and out of the wool – but that was several years ago now. Since then, arthritis had crippled her hands so badly that she would never again be able to enjoy the sewing, embroidery and knitting she'd learned at her mother's knee.

"Not really," sighed Arthur. "She's in constant pain. She takes pills all day long, but none of them seem to help much."

"Is it easier now you've set up a bed for her in the front room?"

"Definitely. She got so frustrated when she couldn't manage the stairs."

Alice watched her mother as she shuffled out to the bathroom, grabbing surfaces to steady herself whenever she could. "She has always been so busy bustling around sorting out everything for everyone."

"She's a good girl," agreed Arthur, his eyes misting over. "God blessed me when he sent Daisy my way."

Alice linked her arm through his. "Just call me, Dad. If you need anything for her, or just a bit of a break yourself, call me."

But Arthur wasn't really listening. He was remembering the day fifty years ago when a certain cheeky little bird had looked so charming on the handle of his spade that a lovely young lady with auburn curls had stopped to take a closer look – at Wobin and at the spade's owner! Daisy, his Daisy…

Or how the little flower he trod upon,
The daisy, that white-feathered shield of gold,
Followed with wistful eyes the wandering sun
Content if once its leaves were aureoled.

But surely it is something to have been
The best beloved for a little while,
To have walked hand in hand with Love,
And seen His purple wings flit once across thy smile.

Oscar Wilde, "Apologia"

1984

Arthur hooked the plastic bag containing the few things he had just bought at the corner shop over his arm, then crossed the road towards the house. Clicking the gate closed behind him, he turned back, gazing for a while up and down the street. He'd been born here nearly eighty years ago and had honestly never wanted to leave. It was his home.

Dusk was falling. Street lights had begun to glow, and curtains were drawn across windows as families settled down for the evening. Cars jostled for spaces in the narrow street as people arrived home from work. *No one walks nowadays,* thought Arthur. He could just picture himself as a little boy hanging over this gate as he waited for his father to walk back from the dockyard, his metal lunch box swinging in his hand. Arthur's gaze shifted then directly across towards the entrance of the small lane which he'd walked down every day as a boy, to the Victorian school building that long ago had been replaced by a smart new primary school nearer the town centre. And as the street stretched up to the left, his mind was filled with the image of Ernest in his soldier's uniform, marching away to war with Arthur's engraved stone in his pocket…

Shivering at a sudden chilly gust of wind, he put his key in the door and walked through to the back room where Daisy smiled to see him. Arthur kissed the dry skin of her cheek, stroking her hair and cupping her face.

"I've got a tin of sardines for tea."

"I'm not really hungry, dear."

"Maybe not now, but sardines have always been your favourite, so I'm hoping they might smell so delicious you'll try a little at least."

"Not now. Perhaps later." Daisy's small smile was apologetic, and Arthur's heart lurched to see how frail she'd become.

"I'll make a cup of tea then. And the news is about to start." He crossed over to the sideboard to switch on the colour television they'd treated themselves to about five years earlier.

Daisy couldn't be tempted by sardines or anything else that evening, so Arthur drew up a chair beside hers, holding her hand as they watched *Coronation Street* together, a programme they never missed.

Arthur was so engrossed in the storyline that it was a while before he noticed. It wasn't until he felt her hand go limp in his that he turned towards her. She looked odd. He couldn't fathom it at first, but as he watched, the left-hand side of her face began to droop downwards.

"Daisy! Daisy, what's wrong? Speak to me!"

But when she spoke, the words were nonsense. Her mouth was opening and shutting like a baby bird's, but the sounds coming out were strange and her eyes were wide with fear. He didn't know what to do. Who should he call? Alice! He'd ring Alice. She'd know what was needed.

Three hours later, Arthur was sitting in a hospital waiting room with Alice and Tommy at his side. He knew it was bad. He could tell from the expression on the doctor's face as he'd taken the children to one side earlier to explain to them quietly about their mother's condition. The nurses were just going to make her comfortable, he'd said, and then the family could go in and sit with her.

They sat there for most of the night, willing her to know they were there and that she wasn't alone. The droop in her face was very pronounced now, and she was ghostly white.

"She doesn't look like Mum with her face like that," whispered Tommy.

"She *is* our mum though – our dear, very loved mum…" breathed Alice.

"She's not going to come home again, is she?" Arthur's voice was bleak and toneless.

Alice turned toward him then, taking his hand gently in her own. "It was a massive stroke, Dad. The doctor said we must prepare ourselves for the worst."

And just as morning light began to creep around the ward curtains, Daisy's breath became slower and slower until at last she breathed no more. Arthur watched as the tense muscles in her face relaxed and smoothed.

"She's at peace," he said quietly. "God will care for her now."

He didn't cry. His parents had taught him not to cry in public. But his dearest companion, his best friend, his beloved wife Daisy was no longer alive – and life held no meaning for him without her.

❦

As long as I can
I will look at this world for both of us.
As long as I can,

I will laugh with the birds,
I will sing with the flowers,
I will pray to the stars for both of us.

Sascha Wagner, "For Both of Us"

Arthur made his very best wreath for his wife. He wound long strands of speckled ivy and feathery ferns into the shape of a heart, and then spread blooms among the greenery: small white roses, the family's flower of remembrance, along with simple cream-coloured daisies with their heart of gold. He could just see the top of the wreath as he walked behind the coffin with Alice at his side. *I hope that wreath doesn't fall off,* he thought. *That would never do at all.*

The church was full. As he glanced along each side of the pew, he spotted friends old and young, dressed in black, their faces pale and sombre.

I would like to have worn the yellow and brown striped jumper Daisy knitted for me, he thought as he moved into the front aisle. *She'd have liked that. She always wanted to cuddle me when I wore it, because the wool was so soft. I'd like to put my arms around you now, my love, lying alone in that box. Don't be scared – not as scared as I am at the thought of living without you. And don't forget you are loved, always and forever.*

They went into the church hall for the wake, and Arthur was dimly aware of groups of people greeting old friends, chatting together and helping themselves to the wonderful buffet Alice had prepared for the occasion. He listened to their words of condolence. He nodded and smiled as yet another well-meaning friend gave him advice on how to cope with bereavement because they'd "been through exactly the same thing" themselves.

And then it was over. With care and concern Alice settled him back home – and then he was alone. Opening the back door, he walked slowly down the path to sit on the old garden bench. Then, as the sun set around him, he buried his head in his hands and cried.

1986

Arthur's Garden

The Lord God planted a garden
In the first white days of the world,
And He set there an angel warden
In a garment of light enfurled.

So near to the peace of Heaven,
That the hawk might nest with the wren,
For there in the cool of the even
God walked with the first of men.

And I dream that these garden-closes
With their shade and their sun-flecked sod
And their lilies and bowers of roses,
Were laid by the hand of God.

The kiss of the sun for pardon,
The song of the birds for mirth, –
One is nearer God's heart in a garden
Than anywhere else on earth...

Dorothy Frances Gurney, "God's Garden"

A YEAR AND A half had passed since Daisy's death, but to Arthur that was nothing more than time. A deep melancholy had settled on his shoulders like a heavy mantle on the day she died. He didn't mind. He had shared so many happy times with her, and now he'd come to this, and that was all right.

He went through the motions of picking up the pieces. He spent time with Alice, Tommy and their families. The children were growing fast. Alice and Michael's son Bertie was nineteen now, studying at university in London, and there were high hopes for his younger sister Angela, who was about to take her A-Levels for which excellent results were expected. Tommy and Belinda's two were doing well too. Claire, now eighteen, had recently left school to take up a post in the town library, while big brother Matthew had got an apprenticeship as a tree surgeon. Arthur found himself smiling at the memory of Matthew growing beans in a jam jar when he was a small boy. He'd been so impatient and ham-fisted then – but his fascination with how plants grew and what went on out of sight under the soil became compelling enough to choose a job where he would always be working outside with plants and trees. Perhaps, thought Arthur, he might turn his hand to gardening one day. Time would tell.

Gardening, though, was Arthur's earthly salvation. It made sense of every day, and shaped the year ahead so that he always had something to look forward to: the first buds of spring, green shoots from the seeds he'd sown, blossoms on the apple tree, bedding flowers in startling colour, leaves falling in glorious autumn hues, the red berries on the holly bush as Christmas came.

A couple of months earlier, the family had helped Arthur celebrate his eightieth birthday. It had been a small affair, a meal at a nice local pub and a birthday cake at home. Thank goodness they had only asked him to blow out eight candles, one for each decade of his life. This wretched breathlessness, which kept him awake at night and had him coughing by day, meant that to count his candles in decades rather than years suited him perfectly now.

Towards the end of the meal, Tommy had unveiled the special gift he had made for his father's birthday.

"Dad, you've been working in your garden now for several decades. You've dug it and shaped it, hoed and watered it. You've seen wartime dogfights in the sky above it. You filled every corner with vegetables when food supplies were short, then turned it back again into a miracle of flowers and shrubs that never look the same from one year – or even one day – to the next. You have created a little of God's heaven in your garden for us all to enjoy. So this is for you, to mark all you have achieved."

Arthur pulled back the wrapping to reveal a wooden sign with tall supports on either side. On the front were carved just two words: "Arthur's Garden".

Arthur was touched beyond words, and later that day Tommy helped him position the sign at the house end of the garden, where he could see it from the chair in the back room window. Looking at it, Arthur was filled with a deep sense of pride – and responsibility too, because he was determined that "Arthur's Garden" should always look its best, even if he was feeling a bit under the weather himself. That challenge was nothing less than a pleasure. The garden held as much appeal for him as it ever did.

His days fell into a comfortable pattern. He got any domestic chores done during the morning before sitting down to watch the lunchtime news while he ate a sandwich washed down with a cup of tea. Often, he'd nod off to sleep as he sat there, waking some time later with a start to stare at the clock on the mantelpiece. That would be his cue to head out for a few hours of work in the garden before he made another cup of tea to drink as he sat on the bench to watch the sun go down.

He'd been meaning to tidy up the sideboard for ages, but had put it off because he knew that inside that piece of sturdy oak furniture was a treasure trove of memories – christening candles, wedding certificates, cherished letters and faded photos of years gone by. But that wet morning when he felt he really couldn't put off the job any longer, he found it wasn't sadness he felt, but a deep warm glow as each memento recalled poignant moments of times gone by.

Arthur's fingers rested on a brittle piece of card that had been pushed to the back corner of one of the drawers. Pulling it out, he looked down at the stern-faced picture of his brother Ernest, smartly dressed in his army uniform, in a formal studio photograph taken in 1916, just a few days before he left for the Front. And in the pocket of that uniform, thought Arthur, was the small polished stone that he had lovingly engraved for the big brother he adored. "Come home" – that was Arthur's message. Ernest hadn't come home, of course, but Arthur had never *left* home. His heart was here, where he'd been surrounded by the love of parents, brothers, sisters, children, grandchildren, nieces, nephews, friends and neighbours.

And he thought then of his old friend Jesus, the one he'd thought had deserted him, but whose quiet presence he'd sensed so clearly alongside him down the years.

"When I'm not here," Arthur said out loud, "when you've taken me home to be with Daisy again, look after them all, won't you? Thank you for the blessing of each and every one of them. Bless them as you've always blessed me."

And in the silence, Arthur felt that quiet presence again. He was not alone. He was never alone.

Tommy and Belinda hosted the family Christmas that year, so Alice and Michael called in to collect Arthur on their way over to lunch. There was great excitement when they arrived as the young cousins noisily greeted each other, the men disappeared with drinks to chat in the living room, and Belinda and Alice opened a bottle of white wine to keep them going as they peeled vegetables from Tommy's own garden.

The dinner was magnificent, especially Alice's home-made Christmas pudding made from the family recipe passed down through generations of mothers and daughters. And then they all found a seat around the Christmas tree to open presents. Arthur sat back in a comfy armchair in the corner, smiling at the exclamations of delight, the hugs and the infectious laughter as presents were torn open and the carpet was covered in a mountain of bright Christmas paper.

Tom had found a lovely old gardening book for his father, and Arthur turned its pages with delight as he read some of the traditional garden wisdoms he remembered his own father passing on to him. He looked forward to reading it properly when he got home that evening.

It was eight o'clock before Alice and Michael dropped him off, hugging him fondly before they said their goodbyes. Arthur made himself a cup of tea, then settled down in the back room chair as he opened the book on his lap.

Half an hour later, he was feeling a bit queasy. Not surprising really after all the rich food he'd eaten that day. But indigestion was something he'd never really suffered from, and this was so uncomfortable that he got up to fetch himself a dose of Milk of Magnesia from the dark blue bottle Daisy had always kept in the bathroom cabinet. *That will work soon*, he thought, settling back into the chair to read more of his book.

He became totally engrossed, coming across friends old and new in the blooms and plants the book mentioned. Finally, he leaned back, his mind full of flowers and how he might use them in his garden, as his eyelids grew heavy and finally closed.

Down this garden path, slowly I make my way.
Not wanting to startle my thoughts, bounding about
in play.

Memories old, some newly dreamt yet to bear their fruit.
Search a quiet place to sit among my many thoughts of you.

They weave their way in sunlit dance, merriment
amid the blooms.
With them I lay another day, until amber skies kiss the moon.

Bev Smith, "Amid the Blooms"

The doctor said that Arthur's heart attack had been swift and probably over before he realized. Two weeks later, at the church where he'd been baptized, married, and now was to be buried, Alice cleared her throat nervously as she stepped up to the pulpit. She looked out at a sea of familiar faces. Wilf was looking pale and shaken at the end of one of the rows, between several pews that were filled with neighbours, work mates who had known Arthur at the yard, and family members who had gathered from far and wide. Lily, the eldest of Arthur's siblings, was too frail now at the age of eighty-seven to leave her care home to come to his funeral, and Ada had died several years earlier. Dick and his wife Audrey had travelled down from London, to sit alongside an ashen-faced Bo.

Taking a deep breath, Alice began to read:

Our father kept a garden,
A garden of the heart;
He planted all the good things
That gave our lives their start.

He turned us to the sunshine,
And encouraged us to dream:
Fostering and nurturing
the seeds of self-esteem.

And when the winds and rain came,
He protected us enough;
But not too much because he knew
We'd stand up strong and tough.

His constant good example
Always taught us right from wrong;
Markers for our pathway that will last
a lifetime long.

We are our father's garden;
We are his legacy.

Thank you, Dad. We love you.

Epilogue

It was heart-breaking to sell a house that had been in the family for so long, but as there was no one able to take it on, after six months Tommy and Alice agreed that there was nothing for it but to put their father's home up for sale. A young couple with a small baby bought it. The husband was a DIY enthusiast who saw the house as a "doer-upper". Within a year, every room had been gutted and redesigned. The attic was turned into a study, and the cellar became a playroom for their young son.

The coal depot that for so many years had stood across the back lane had long gone, and the land had been redeveloped to become a new estate of starter homes. The young couple were pleased to see this, hoping it might mean some small playmates nearby for their little boy.

The surprisingly beautiful garden they'd discovered at the back of the house when they first saw it had been an important factor in their decision to sign on the dotted line straight away. However, as the months passed, and neither of them had any experience of gardening, the back yard became overgrown and uncared for. Eventually, the new owners thought there was nothing for it but to concrete it, building in a sandpit for their son, a rotary washing line and a barbecue for sunny weekends.

But before the house had been sold, Tommy had got to work with his secateurs and potting compost. He had taken down the greenhouse pane by pane, reconstructing it in the back corner of his own garden. He'd dug out rooted clumps of plants, shrubs and roses – especially Ernest's white rose, which he carefully removed to its new home along the fence that Belinda could see from her kitchen window. And in the flowerbed directly in front of their large patio doors, Tommy dug in the sign that read "Arthur's Garden".

And on the morning when the first frost breathed its silvery coating across the lawn, Tommy drew back the bedroom curtains to see a visitor in the garden.

Sitting on the sign, his head cocked to look Tommy straight in the eye, sat Wobin. They stared at each other like old friends for just a moment, before Wobin threw back his head and chirruped to welcome the morning sun.

Dates and Details

Tom Freeman (1877–1927): married Emily in 1895. By 1922 had had a fall and couldn't manage work.

Emily Freeman (1878–1965).

Tom and Emily's children

Thomas (1896): only lived one day.

Lily (born 1897): married Laurie in July 1917, first son Ronald Ernest.

Ernest (1898–1916): killed at Flanders.

Twins (born 1900), ALICE (stillborn) and ADA: Ada married Albert in 1931; lived just up the road from Arthur with their two boys, Jack (born 1925) and Freddie (born 1927).

Richard (Dick) (born 1902): moved to London to work in 1922, aged twenty; married Audrey there in 1925, aged twenty-three.

John (born 1904): started working at the local gasworks, aged eighteen. He'd emigrated to Canada by the time Arthur and Daisy married in June 1933.

Arthur (3rd April 1906 – Christmas Day 1986): started working as a carpenter in the dockyard in 1922, aged sixteen. Married Daisy in June 1933, when he was twenty-seven and she was twenty-three. Alice Emily, daughter born April 1934; Thomas Ernest (Tommy) born in spring 1939.

Elsie (born 1909): bridesmaid at Lily and Laurie's wedding in 1916 when she was seven; started work, aged sixteen, as a typist in Morrison's Solicitors; married Sam Morrison in 1935 – no children.

Harry (born 1911): married Hetty, daughter of a work mate at the Coal Board. After the war, he took an office job at the coal depot.

Bo (born October 1913): christened Robert, but two-year-old Harry couldn't say that name and called him Bo, and that stuck. Left home by June 1933 (Arthur's wedding) into digs near Gravesend, where he worked on the Thames barges. Came back from war having been a Japanese prisoner-of-war. Married Dora in 1947, widow of Frank, who was killed on D-Day. Twin girls, Christine and Rosemary, born in March 1939 so they were nearly ten years old when David was born in January 1949.

Arthur and Daisy's children

Alice (born April 1934): married Michael, Deputy Head at the local comprehensive, in July 1966. Their children: Bertie (baptized Robert) in 1967, and Angela born in 1969.

Tommy (born Thomas Ernest in spring 1939): married Belinda in 1965. Worked as a Post Office engineer. Their children: Matthew, born 1966 (as an adult, got an apprentice as a tree surgeon) and Claire, born 1968, shy and bookish, got a job in the local library after leaving school at eighteen.

Acknowledgments

Scripture quotations are taken from The Authorized (King James) Version. Rights in the Authorized Version are vested in the Crown. Reproduced by permission of the Crown's patentee, Cambridge University Press.

p. 59 "When the Red, Red Robin (Comes Bob, Bob, Bobbin' Along)" by Harry M. Woods. Copyright © 1926 Harry M. Woods. Used by permission of Bourne Company and The Songwriters Guild of America.

p. 77 The extract from "The Diehards" by Ruth Pitter, from her Collected Poems, is reproduced by permission of Enitharmon Editions, www.enitharmon.co.uk.

pp. 80–81 "A Widow's Weeds" in *Peacock Pie* by Walter de la Mare, published by Constable and Company. Later published in *The Complete Poems of Walter de la Mare* (1975). Copyright © 1913 Walter de la Mare. Used by permission of The Society of Authors.

p. 93 Extract from *Glory! To the Flowers* by Maggie Steincrohn Davis, illustrated by Cara Raymaker, published by Heartsong Books. Copyright © 1995 Maggie Steincrohn Davis. Used by permission of the author. CaringInRememberedWays.org.

p. 103 "Desire" in *The World Will Follow Joy: Turning Madness into Flowers* (New Poems), by Alice Walker, published by The New Press. Copyright © 2014 Alice Walker/ The New Press. Used by permission of The New Press and Joy Harris Literary Agency.

p. 131 "CHERRY PINK AND APPLE BLOSSOM WHITE" Words by Mack David and Jacques Larue, Music by Louiguy © 1951 SIDOMUSIC B LIECHTI ET CIE (PRS) All rights on behalf of SIDOMUSIC B LIECHTI ET CIE administered by WARNER/CHAPPELL MUSIC LTD

p. 149 "Gardener's Complaint" in *Round and Round the Garden* by Marian French, published by Angus & Robertson. Copyright © 1993 HarperCollins Australia Pty Limited. Used by permission of HarperCollins Australia Pty Limited.

p. 166 "One Perfect Rose," copyright 1926, renewed © 1954 by Dorothy Parker; from *THE PORTABLE DOROTHY PARKER* by Dorothy Parker, edited by Marion Meade. Used by permission of Viking Books, an imprint of Penguin Publishing Group, a division of Penguin Random House LLC.All rights reserved.

p. 176 "Why Don't We Grow Weeds" by Eunice Perkins. Used by permission of the author.

p. 187 "For Both of Us" in *The Poems of Sascha Wagner*, published by Tennessee Valley Publishing. Copyright © 2008 The Compassionate Friends. Used by permission of The Compassionate Friends.

p. 198 "Amid the Blooms" by Bev Smith. Used by permission of the author.